CULINARY MAGIC *at the* REGENERATIVE DESIGN INSTITUTE

Creating community through food, farm and permaculture

by CARIN McKAY

Ordering Information:
Visit www.culinarymagic.com

Design by Caroline Wallace

ISBN 978-0-615-77646-0

First Edition
Printed in China

dedications

To Great Great Grandma Lola Greer, who showed me the power of handmade things through her beautiful aprons and quilts.

To Great Grandma Opal Myrtue, who taught me how to make a root cellar apple pie.

To Grandma Mary Kroll, who always has fresh-baked homemade cookies on hand, just in case.

And to my mom, Patricia Anne Kroll McKay Adi, who taught me about the joy of food.

TABLE *of* CONTENTS

MEAL BLESSING

The silver rain, the golden sun
The field where scarlet poppies run,
And all the rustling of the wheat
Is in the food that we shall eat.

And so with grateful heart I feel,
When I sit down to every meal
That I am eating wind and sun,
And fields where scarlet poppies run.

Alice C. Henderson

Adapted from Claude Monet's poem,
"Oat and Poppy Field"

CULINARY MAGIC

When I talk about culinary magic, I'm not talking about having the right ingredients and knowing how to mix them together. I'm talking about lineage. I'm talking about people. I'm talking about what emerges when you consciously weave together community, history, health, nature, and a real enjoyment of where you are.

In my life, my first sense of culinary magic started with my mom. Her passion for homemade bread, garden-grown tomatoes, and world cuisine blended perfectly with her mid-western roots, and rubbed off on me in the way I approach food. To my mom, food was home. Food was passion. Food was love.

As a child growing up in Mendocino, California, I also grew up in the wild beauty of nature. Nature was ever-present there, and my town was steeped in a culture of art, non-commercialism, and do-it-your-self. Mendocino was not the big city. We didn't even have a stoplight. The pace of life was slower, and the 'environment' wasn't a political movement to get behind, but something that we thought about as a regular part of how we lived. As an art town, Mendocino also had great food, and my first job was in a restaurant there.

By the time I got to college, I knew that preparing food could be treated as an art form (or an Olympic sport), and I understood the chaos of restaurant kitchens. But it was only at college that I started to learn how fun it was to cook for a community. An afternoon spent picking fresh fruit off the trees easily led to many late-night pie-making parties. We had long evenings of making spaghetti where everyone added something to the sauce. Again and again, I saw how food could be the foundation of people coming together and having a really great time.

It was also in college that I began to think about how food is medicine. Having grown up without medical insurance, I was interested in how could I be personally empowered to care for my health. This question led me to study herbal medicine, emotional counseling, wild food foraging, and macrobiotics. I was interested in the idea that we could influence our physical and emotional health through our diets instead of relying on invasive procedures and pharmaceutical drugs.

The lure of this idea led me to New York City, where I met the first of a series of important mentors. Mentors are a vital part of any person's journey, and my story is no different.

At the Institute of Integrative Nutrition (IIN), I had the fortune of meeting Joshua Rosenthal. Joshua was the founder and visionary of IIN, and he taught me how to counsel people around their health and nutrition. I owe my love of this work to Joshua, and I've been lucky to counsel hundreds of people around their physical health and emotional well-being. I eventually became a lecturer at IIN, and led workshops for thousands of people helping them make important connections between their experience of their physical and emotional well-being, and the food they eat.

Upon returning to San Francisco, I met a person who changed (and continues to change) my life as a chef in the very best ways. When I met Teo Weiss, I already had a strong interest in community. But I was still thinking about the kitchen as a place where the food is first, and the people are second. I had been misled to think that restaurant kitchens are places for people who like perfection, people who are driven to excel in their passion of making the very "best" food. And if the days got really long, if feelings got hurt, if tempers ran short—that was just the business.

Teo turned all of this on its head. In Teo's kitchen, people were first, and so was food. They were not mutually exclusive. Community wasn't just something that happened when we served our food, but something we created while we were making the food. Teo showed (and continues to show) me that the dynamic between people in the kitchen matters. It matters to the people and their sense of connection, and it matters to the end result—the quality of the food we make.

There are strong personalities in any kitchen. There are emotions, and flare-ups and really bad days. The idea here is that these things matter (in addition to the food), and the vibe in the kitchen needs conscious attention if you are going to create anything inwardly or outwardly nourishing. Teo continues to be my mentor and collaborator, and I feel lucky to have his influence woven into the very fabric of who I am as a chef.

While my skill as a chef/counselor has been influenced by amazing teachers, no history would be complete without a mention of Penny Livingston and James Stark. My first experience with Penny was in answer to her invitation to come cook at her place for a group of 50 people. The location was at a place called Sky Water Ranch. I made the drive from San Francisco in the 100-degree heat, and arrived at James and Penny's mountain-top ranch exhilarated but tired from the drive.

Penny greeted me warmly and then looked at me with a wide grin. She said, "Uh, well, we were planning on building you a kitchen, but we decided we would let you help design it." For a minute I thought I misheard her. No kitchen? Wait, what? I was expected to cook for a large group of people...with no kitchen?

That night, I served 50 people using a double burner stove out under the stars. The situation was so unusual, I realized there was no point in stressing out. As the week went on, I got to design my outdoor kitchen. The group built us an outdoor structure with a fir branch roof that night, and when it started to rain halfway through the meal, we were happily dry. Later that summer, James built us a brick oven, and soon we were making breads and desserts, outdoors, on the top of the mountain. This zest for nutty adventure struck a chord in me. We somehow knew we had found kindred do-it-yourself spirits in each other, and Penny and James have been wonderful collaborators ever since.

In working with Penny and James, I found a great convergence of my interests in food, health, nature, permaculture, transformational work, and community. Culinary Magic, as a business, began to take shape as a way to integrate so many things I care about.

I have cooked on the top of mountains, under the open sky, in redwood forests, in fancy kitchens, in non-existent kitchens, and in former bomb shelters. I have made bread in brick ovens, woven cattails around salmon, and baked wild boar in the earth. I've baked cookies with solar energy, and made meals for 200 people on an outdoor fire. To me, this is the kind of magic that makes for food that truly nourishes—food that is made for a community to build community, infused with history, intention, irreverence, wackiness, adventure, and connection.

COOKING *at the* REGENERATIVE DESIGN INSTITUTE

The pleasure of fresh still astounds me. I clearly remember the canned peas and TV dinners of my growing up, and the first time my mother brought me a real tomato, sun-ripened on the vine. Red, juicy, flavorful, alive, this tomato was delicious on its own. The power of the experience jolted me awake. It was as though I had been watching the world in black and white, and then suddenly saw things in color for the first time.

To be able to cook now with food that grows 50 feet away from the kitchen is truly a dream. There is nothing like being handed a basket of fresh fava beans that were just picked, a handful of garlic scapes, or a gallon of goat's milk still warm from being hand-milked that morning.

I love being able to walk in the garden and pick edible flowers and handfuls of fresh herbs for tonight's supper. On the farm here, there are eggs, fresh goats milk, abundant herbs, flowers, wild edibles, greens, and the most beautiful lettuces you have ever seen.

Still, for many people, the experience of fresh food still seems like a fairy tale. At RDI, I have had people come to me in tears (literally in tears) about how good the food was and how alive they felt. And while I love the compliments, I also know that when we eat local food from the place it was grown, we are bound to have a powerful experience with our food.

When we see where our food comes from we begin to connect with a sense of place and the rhythms of nature. Something bigger is happening than just tasty food. Eating local, in season food syncs us up with our environment, and when we eat, we are directly taking nature in our bodies. Our experience of being alive physically, emotionally, and mentally begins to come into harmony with the cycles of the earth.

There is a deep connection we are all craving that is met by eating this way. It feels good. It is our birthright to have this kind of connection with our environment. And it is my dream that all people have the opportunity to be connected to their food in this way.

Photos on opposite page >
1. Garden cardoons.
2. Morning time goat care.
3. Morning time at RDI.
4. Lots of fresh honey at the farm.
5. Harvesting fresh kale for today's lunch.

1

2

3

4

5

TRANSFORMING OUR RELATIONSHIP *to* FOOD, FARMING *and* NATURE

This fine spring morning, I hear birds singing, water flowing in the creek, the hiss of a tea kettle getting ready to boil for my morning tea, and the wind rustling through the trees. I see greens in the garden, herbs, berries, budding fruit trees and bees buzzing from flower to flower. The delicate scent of roses, pine, and newly scythed grasses wafts up from the yard below. I feel the warmth of the sun and sea breeze on my skin. I taste the delicious flavors of my breakfast: eggs from our chickens, feta cheese from our goats, homegrown preserves on fresh, warm, homemade bread made from the wild grain we collected last summer and ground only yesterday. I feel full of wonder, gratitude and excitement as I sit on the edge of another day.

I started growing a vision for how to live in an ecologically abundant world about 23 years ago, and I hold this vision for our society as well. We are in an era of global transformation. Our cosmology is changing as we come to realize that our survival is dependent on changing our relationship to creation, the natural world and the planet Earth. This transformation is transcending religion, culture, climate, and consciousness. We are awakening to the realization that we have to change the way we provide for our needs, and the way we develop and care for the land.

This isn't about one person or a few people doing magnanimous tasks to transform society and culture. This is about millions upon millions of people doing simple, ordinary things while making clear and educated decisions. It's about all of us becoming literate about our home and our role in looking after it.

I live at Commonweal Garden, on a 17-acre farm on the Northern California coast. I live close to nature. There are some that tell me that because they live in the city, they don't feel like they can live close to the natural world. In my opinion, this does not have to be true. There are many ways we can connect to our environment. One fundamental way to have a more intimate relationship with the Earth is to look on your plate. What are you eating? Where does your food come from? Do you know the farmer? How much of what you eat is local and in season? Do you have an ideal picture of what the food on your plate should be? Can you create a vision for yourself that includes a healthy relationship with your food (and therefore to the larger world)? A deeper connection to your food can be a pathway to a deeper connection with the Earth.

And that's where I started with my first permaculture course. At that time, I was already growing organic vegetables and flowers and selling them at the local health food store, but this training introduced me to a number of the permaculture ideas: growing your own food, cleaning and harvesting water, developing local non-toxic solutions for shelter. Concepts like "designing with nature", "using onsite resources", cleaning water and soil biologically and finding multiple functions for everything we design in our living systems became part of a new way I viewed the world. Through permaculture, I began to glimpse a way that we humans could co-exist on the planet in a healthy way. These ideas made so much sense at the time, yet conventional western development wasn't utilizing them. Participating with the world in this way develops a sense of how we are connected, how our systems are connected, and how our planet is connected.

And we do need each other. In my opinion, "self sufficiency" isn't the ideal, because doing everything by yourself isn't sustainable. Actually the opposite may be a better option. The saying "many hands make light work" is very true in my long experience. Burly tasks that may seem overwhelming alone can actually be fun when done in community with friends. As we move into the new paradigm, it seems to me that village culture may indeed hold the answer to living well in our modern era. The number of quality relationships we have may turn out to be more valuable than the number of quality "things" that we have.

And contrary to what some may think, a permaculture lifestyle is not expensive. With this lifestyle you can eat the freshest most delicious food, and live well on a low budget. The solutions are here. At our fingertips, we already have the technology and knowhow to grow food without chemicals, to design and build energy systems that are clean and renewable, to build structures without toxins, and to treat each other with respect and compassion. We need to continue honing our skills to provide for our needs in ways that all of creation can thrive in the process.

So I invite you to consider your own life: How do you wake in the morning? How do you sit on the edge of each new day? What do you dream it could be like? How do you relate to the world around you?

–Penny Livingston
Co-Founder RDI

Photo on opposite page >

Artichoke is a thistle. The often maligned thistle is edible, medicinal, and a wonderful insectary. Bees love it because it's pollen tastes like light honey. Thistle holds a beauty that often people fail to see due to it's prickly stickers and potentially invasive quality. Thistle is a soil builder who works to create balance, loosening the soil and accumulating much needed minerals for the soil. Penny often leaves thistle in her garden as the gophers prefer thistle roots to lettuce plants.

how to
COOK A COOK....

"Show me your scars," the head chef asked me when I was being interviewed for the job. I promptly rolled up my sleeves and showed him the variety of small scars I had on my arms and hands. He hired me on the spot. The scars didn't necessarily get me the job, but they certainly clinched the deal. My burns and cuts told him I was a motivated person and a dedicated cook—dedicated beyond all reason.

As a general rule, cooks are ruled by passion. Some might even say we're a bit "touched." Why else would we stay up late perfecting a leg of lamb, or tattoo measurement conversions on our stomachs, or sleep with a stack of cookbooks by our beds? Our obsession with food goes way beyond any paycheck.

And while we happily talk about the importance of cooking with fresh ingredients, we rarely talk about the importance of cooking with healthy cooks. Put simply, cooks are not just food-making machines. But the cook world is renown for being hard on its people.

The daily rigors of kitchen work can take a real toll on cooks' bodies. The hours are long, the working environments are dangerous (and sometimes yucky), stress levels run high, people can be emotionally difficult and feel justified yelling at each other, and the pay is ridiculously low. In the restaurant world, cooks regularly use uppers or downers to increase their alertness, deal with the pressure, or try to relax.

But we never think to ask: Do we really want to eat some fancy food that was made by someone who is anxious and under a lot of stress? Do we really want to eat a meal made by someone so tired or emotionally worked up that he or she has to use substances to stay focused or calm?

The vibe in the kitchen definitely affects the quality of the food. It is important that we cooks are getting along with each other. We need make sure that we are taking care of our health, and that we are relaxed when we're in the process of making our food. The key here is balance. If someone in my kitchen (including me) is stressed out or getting cut or burned, that's a sure sign something or someone is not in balance.

Maintaining balance, by the way, is not easy. It means holding all the time pressure, the desire for things to be perfect, the worry that they won't be, and keeping the bigger picture in sight. Cooking has taught me that it really does all work out in the end. Cooking teaches me to breathe. It teaches me to stay as focused and relaxed as possible...no matter what happens.

So how do you cook a cook?

The first way is check-ins. I have regular check-ins with all the staff. In our check-ins, we give appreciations to each other, and we give feedback on how to best improve the flow of the kitchen. This is a valuable way for each person to express him or herself, and to be heard and seen as a person.

The culture of a kitchen is important, so I try to create an atmosphere that can bring out the best in each person and their abilities as a cook. I see our work together as a way to enhance the goals and dreams of each chef, and to facilitate his or her journey as a human being.

I welcome discussion, collaboration, even disagreements. I bring humor and a sense of play. I also try to insist that we support one another when the inevitable mishap happens. Too often the person who spilled the rice or burnt the soup is feeling awful and alone in a corner somewhere. Rallying as a team in these moments creates an interconnected and supportive environment. And let's face it, we are often in unusual situations, and while the stress of making things work can be a test, it is a great opportunity to get to know each other.

I often say the kitchen can be a "cruel mistress." If you don't pay attention, even for a second, you can get hurt. In this way, I think of the kitchen as a teacher. The kitchen teaches me to pay attention, to be mindful of intentions, and to be present with what I am doing.

For me, being a cook is about being a creator. It's about being able to make my personal version of a Tibetan sand painting—a task that takes hours of focus and intention to create—and yet with a brush of a hand, is gone. This is true with how I approach the craft, how I create my food, and how I care for the people who work alongside me to make it.

COOKING *for a* COMMUNITY...

Sharing food together is one way we build community. The food we eat goes into our bodies, and becomes our blood, our organs, our brain. Food ultimately effects our thoughts and feelings. In a subtle way, eating the same food puts us in harmony with each other.

Eating in community means that everyone is at the table. We are all different, and this is definitely reflected in what we eat. For some of us, it can be a big deal to temporarily give up some of our individual food preferences to eat together in community. Giving this up can be a real act of vulnerability. And as a cook, there are so many different food needs, diets, and cultural differences to carefully consider.

I cook meat, vegetarian, vegan, and gluten free food at nearly every meal. This tends to cover the majority of people. However, I also meet folks who are raw food people, others who are on a no garlic/onion diet, and still others on an all-animal protein diet. There are those with deadly allergies, and others who are changing their diet week by week. How to cook a single meal for everyone with all these different diets? What defines a healthy meal?

In my career, I have watched a lot of dietary trends come and go, from fat-free diets to all-meat diets, to the wonders of oat-bran. Some of these diets work, and some are found to be bunk later on. New information on "what we should eat" seems to come out every week. I navigate this onslaught with a simple rule: if a food has been around for 100 years or more, it's more likely to be better for our health than something created within the last century with modern day processes.

For me, it's all about balance. A balanced meal means having good quality protein, fat, and complex carbohydrates at every meal. In other words, I like to have protein (vegetarian or meat), a whole grain, sweet vegetables, green vegetables, and good quality oil/fat in every meal. In general, when I include all of these components, most people will have a feeling of satisfaction.

At RDI, we get students from all different backgrounds and from all parts of the world. Using my global travel experiences and the variety of produce we grow at RDI, I can incorporate many ideas into world cuisine. I cook Italian, Japanese, Southern USA, Brazilian, Indian, Thai, Chinese, Moroccan, Syrian, Italian, Spanish, Greek, and Mexican, all with a Californian influence. I also incorporate foraged food when I can. With this variety of flavors, people are bound to have at least one, if not several, meals that they love and give them the feeling of home. While I am cooking these different styles of food, I remember my principles of what makes a good meal: a protein, a grain, a sweet vegetable, a leafy green, and some good quality fat.

More subtly, I think about digestion. Digestion begins in the eyes, ears, and nose even before the food is on our plate, so we cooks talk about the food we make, and share the lineage of where it came from before the meal. Letting our guests see who made their meal and inviting them to hear our journey, helps everyone experience a connection to their food and where it came from.

INGREDIENTS *for* LIVING *from the* HEART

Over the years, we have been exploring at RDI the "ingredients" for a holistic diet for living, a diet that enables us to lead a more vibrant and abundant life on the inside—as well as on the outside. We believe that fostering inner health is one of the first steps towards creating resilient communities.

Please enjoy this recipe that immerged from our Ecology of Leadership program. Trust your intuition on the amounts, and by all means, feel free to add ingredients to satisfy your particular tastes.

GRATITUDE

Starting our day with a focus on the things we are thankful for opens our hearts, deepens our connection to the natural world including those around us, and helps to quiet the mind. What are we thankful for? How can we bring gratitude into more moments of the day?

CURIOSITY

Curiosity unleashes our creativity and frees our imagination. We discover our gifts and our unique path in life by tracking what lights us up. How do we re-kindle the fire of our childhood curiosity? Can we imagine the world in which we wish to live?

SELF-LOVING

Self-love is an appreciation of who we are. How can we see ourselves as precious, exquisite manifestations of the creative force of the universe? How can we hold ourselves as divine beings?

FORGIVENESS

When we forgive ourselves or we forgive others, we become free to live from our hearts. What are we ready to forgive that would allow us to love ourselves more? What can we let go of today that will deepen our connection to those around us?

ACCEPTANCE

Acceptance is about seeing what is, not what we wish was true. But it does not mean that we stop dreaming. How can we accept what is in order to powerfully generate our dream for the world in which we wish to live?

SURRENDER

Surrender to the unknown has been described as "living as an empty cup", but it is tempting to want to cling to and defend what we know. Rather than dwelling in and defending all that we know, how can we be at home with the unknown? How can we trust that it is all right to not have all the answers?

VULNERABILITY

When we are open and vulnerable, we become connected more deeply with others. It isn't easy, but the fruits of vulnerability are infinite. Vulnerability unlocks the full potential of being alive and inspires others to share deeply from their own hearts. How can we learn to share what we really feel? How might our willingness to be vulnerable transform our lives and enable us to live from our hearts?

Bon Appétit! –James Stark, *Co-Founder RDI*

the REGENERATIVE DESIGN INSTITUTE

The Regenerative Design Institute (RDI) is a non-profit educational organization with the vision that all people can live in a mutually enhancing relationship with the earth. We envision a world in which people, inspired by nature, create and maintain healthy and abundant livelihoods that enhance fertility and biodiversity on the planet. We envision humans as a positive, healing presence on Earth, creating more abundance on the planet than would be possible without them.

RDI is deeply grateful to be located at Commonweal Garden, a beautiful 17 acre coastal site in Bolinas, Ca. The garden has been transformed into a large-scale living classroom and demonstration center for permaculture and regenerative design. RDI hosts hundreds of visitors and course participants every year and offers a wide array of courses in permaculture, nature connection, leadership, herbal studies, re-skilling, and more.

Our mission is to serve as a catalyst for a transformation in the way humans relate to the natural world. Through our programs and courses, we provide the skills and technology people need to become community leaders and create healthy solutions to the current environmental crisis. By training and empowering skilled designers, farmers, trades-people, educators, facilitators and community leaders, RDI demonstrates that we can design and develop models worldwide to address human needs while simultaneously regenerating the earth, making it more fertile and diverse in the process.

For information on The Regenerative Design Institute visit our website at www.regenerativedesign.org.

Photo on opposite page >

We live in harmony with the bees. We help each other. We look after them, provide homes for them and protect them. In turn they help pollinate our fruit trees, recieving much needed food in the form of pollen and nectar from our gardens. In spring and summer they provide us with wonderful fresh honey and beeswax. We always leave more than enough honey for them plus we give them more space to make more honey and lay more eggs. It's a perfect symbiotic relationship!

HOW TO USE THIS BOOK

In this book, there are recipes for the omnivore, vegetarian, vegan, and gluten free. If you see a recipe that doesn't seem like it is for you, look at the bottom of the recipe for options on how to modify it. Since I cook for communities where we are all eating the same meal together, most of my recipes are very easy to convert to suit many people's dietary needs.

As a person who constantly breaks the rules while cooking, I recommend that you follow a recipe exactly once, and then make adjustments to your liking the next time you cook it. I've found that when we follow a recipe, we get the precise knowledge of what it takes to make a certain dish. Following a recipe forces us out of our culinary ruts. And yet, it isn't until we go "off recipe" that we begin to create our food in a new way.

More importantly, please have fun. Try new things out. Make a big mess. Burn some stuff. Invite people over. Learn about what you love to make.

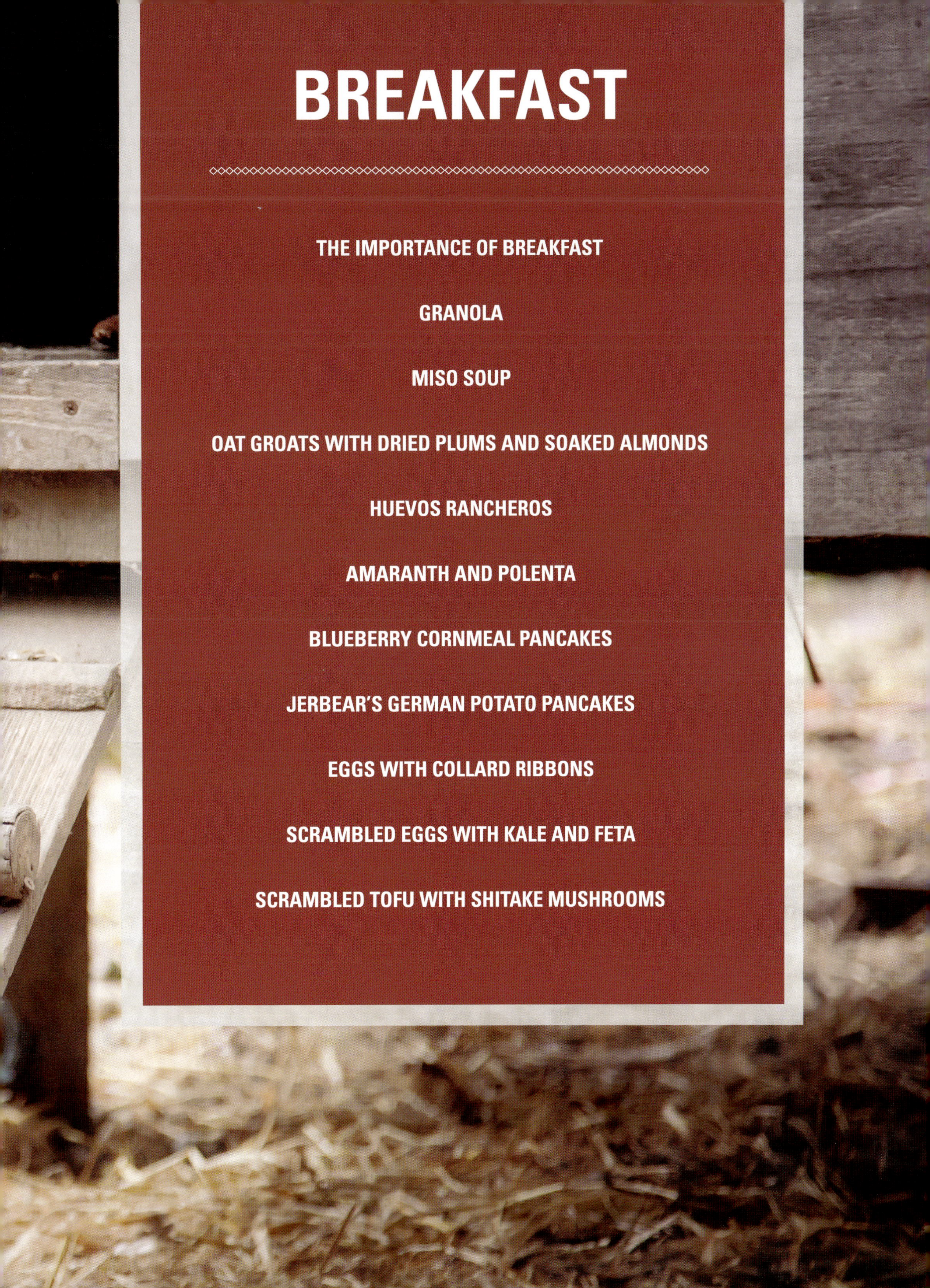

BREAKFAST

the IMPORTANCE *of* BREAKFAST

We have all heard it. Breakfast is the most important meal of the day. But is it really true? Yes. After a night of sleeping where we don't eat for several hours, we are literally breaking our "fast" with breakfast. This first meal sets the tone for our day, and gives us the vital energy we need to do our creative work in the world.

When a person comes to me saying that he or she is feeling depressed, having mood swings, or struggling with weight, the first question I ask is, "Are you eating a wholesome breakfast in the morning?" Most of the time, the answer is no.

And the pattern is always easy to recognize. When people skimp on breakfast, the result is to overeat later in the day, and to rely on stimulants for energy. But it doesn't have to be this way.

Breakfast is a meal that should be sustaining, a meal that can help you regulate your blood sugar throughout the day. If you want consistent energy and stable emotions all day long, having a nutritious, regular breakfast is the way to start. It is your simple daily habits that will have the most impact on your health over time.

A good breakfast should be in the morning. The timing is important because we are living creatures who depend on food at regular times for our bodies to function best. Breakfast before 9:00 am is all right, but by 8:00 am is better. Your breakfast can have good quality fats, protein, as well as carbohydrates in it. Ideally breakfast is an actual meal. And no, coffee with a little cream (fat) and sugar (carbohydrates) does not count.

A good breakfast also includes hydration. Water, green tea, non-caffeinated teas are hydrating. Coffee is dehydrating. If you don't eat breakfast in a regular way, see what happens if you have something wholesome and nourishing in the morning every day for a month. Notice how you feel throughout the day. See what happens when you include hydration in the morning. Experiment.

HOMEMADE GRANOLA

It's so easy to make homemade granola, and your own granola will be much better than anything you can get in the store. The secret to this recipe is once you put the granola in the pans to bake, not to stir it until it is completely cool.

6 tablespoons sesame seeds
6 tablespoons sunflower seeds
½ cup cashews or almonds, sliced
4 cups uncooked rolled oats
⅔ cup unsweetened shredded coconut
¼ teaspoon sea salt
⅔ cup rice or sunflower oil
⅓ cup honey
1 teaspoon vanilla
½ cup dried cranberries or raisins (put on the granola after it comes out of the oven)

Measure and mix together all the dry ingredients (except the dried fruit). Heat up honey with oil and vanilla on low heat and then pour it over dry ingredients. Mix well.

Spread evenly on a baking sheet and cook at 300 degrees for 45-50 minutes until medium brown. Do not stir or mix the granola on pan. When the granola comes out of the oven, sprinkle the cranberries on top. Do not stir. Let cool, and scrape the granola off the pan with a spatula into satisfying chunks.

OPTION

To make a gluten free version, substitute quinoa flakes for oats. Oats technically don't have gluten in them, but are often grown near crops that do.

MISO SOUP *with* CARROTS *and* GINGER

Miso is full of healthy flora that support our digestive system. Miso soup is excellent for breakfast with a piece of sourdough bread and tahini on top. Miso is hydrating after a long night of sleep. I have miso soup anytime of the day, and breakfast is no exception. Make sure you get the miso that's sold in the refrigerator section, as it is still alive and not pasteurized. At the farm, we gather fresh wakame seaweed off the coast. You can get wakame at most health food stores or forage it yourself.

2 strips of dried wakame seaweed, about ½ inch wide
2½ cups water
1 cup sliced carrot
½ onion sliced in half moons
¼ block tofu cut in small cubes
1 tablespoon grated ginger
1 tablespoon sweet white miso mashed with 2 tablespoons water
1 scallion, sliced

Soak wakame in water for 10 minutes. Discard soak water. Bring 2½ cups fresh water to boil. Add carrots and wakame and simmer for a few minutes. Add onions and tofu and cook longer. Cook until vegetables are soft, but not mushy. Add diluted miso and ginger. Adjust miso to taste (you may like it more salty). Turn off heat. You do not want to bring miso to a boil, as it will hurt all the good bacteria. Garnish with scallions.

OPTIONS

Add winter squashes, corn, cabbage, radishes, green beans, or other kinds of miso. Serves 2-4.

OAT GROATS *with* STEWED DRIED PLUMS *and* SOAKED ALMONDS

Oat groats are different than the rolled oats we get in the store. They are a whole food and so delicious. When you cook them, they become creamy and smooth, as do the dried plums. Oats are one of the great calming foods for our digestion and nervous system, and when you soak the almonds overnight, you will find they are easier to digest. This dish requires you prepare it the night before.

3 cups water
½ cup oat groats
¼ teaspoon sea salt
6 dried plums (prunes)
¼ cup almonds

The night before, bring water, oat groats and salt to a boil in a pot with a heavy lid. Reduce heat and boil for 5 minutes. Remove from heat, cover the pot and lid with a towel, and let sit overnight. While the oat groats are cooling, put ¼ cup almonds in water to cover and let sit overnight.

The next morning, add a little hot water to the oat groats, stir, and heat up.

While the oat groats are heating, put the dried plums in a saucepan with ½ cup water. Bring to a simmer, cover, and cook for 10 minutes, or until the dried plums are soft.

To serve, put the cooked oat groats in a bowl and top with 3 stewed dried plums and 2 tablespoons of soaked nuts. You can add your favorite milk and sweetener if you wish. Serves 2-3.

A field of amaranth growing in front of a handmade cordwood house.

the BEST HUEVOS RANCHEROS

4 corn tortillas
Olive oil
Sea salt
1 cup cooked black, pinto, or refried beans
1 teaspoon cumin powder
1 cup fire-roasted salsa
4 eggs
4 tablespoons crumbled feta
¼ red onion, sliced thin

Preheat oven to 350 degrees. With a pastry brush, brush both sides of each corn tortilla with olive oil and sprinkle with salt. Cook in oven for 10 minutes until the tortillas are not all the way crispy, but close. They will crisp up when you take them outside of the oven.

In a saucepan, heat up beans on the stove, add cumin and salt to taste. Pour salsa into skillet. Heat and let simmer. Make four little wells in the salsa, and crack an egg into each well. Cover the eggs and let simmer until the egg is cooked to your desired done-ness. I like it when the egg is firm, but still runny in the middle (about 2 minutes). With a spatula, remove an egg (surrounded by salsa) and place on a crispy tortilla. Top with black beans, feta and red onion. Serves 2-4.

AMARANTH *and* POLENTA

Amaranth is one of the highest protein-rich grains around. By combining amaranth with corn (polenta), all essential amino acids are completely represented in this dish. Creamy and delicious, this recipe is a hit with hot cereal lovers who want something different from oatmeal.

¼ cup of amaranth
¼ cup of polenta
2 cups of water
¼ teaspoon sea salt

Bring water and grains to a boil. Simmer, add sea salt, cover and cook for 20-25 minutes. Stir occasionally to keep the mixture from sticking to the pot. Add more water if necessary. Top with apple butter, raisins, toasted pumpkin seeds and your favorite milk. Serves 2.

BLUEBERRY CORNMEAL PANCAKES

I love pancakes, but sometimes they make me feel flat for hours afterwards. To offset this, I like to add something more substantial than just wheat flour (cornmeal). In this recipe, you can use fresh or frozen fruit, fresh bananas, and walnuts. The key to this recipe is beating the egg whites until they are nice and fluffy.

1 ¼ cup white spelt flour or all-purpose flour
1 teaspoon baking powder
3 ½ tablespoons sugar
1 ½ teaspoons baking soda
½ teaspsoon salt
1 cup cornmeal
2 cups buttermilk
3 egg yolks
3 tablespoons unsalted butter, melted
3 egg whites
1 cup blueberries

Sift together all the dry ingredients. Separate the egg yolks from the egg whites, beat egg whites until stiff and set them aside. Mix together the buttermilk, egg yolks, and melted butter with your dry ingredients. Fold in egg whites.

Pour ¼ cup batter onto greased hot griddle, sprinkle with 2 tablespoons blueberries on each pancake, and cook until bubbles start to form on top. Flip. With pancakes, I always find that it takes a few sacrifices to the pancake deities before I get the temperature all worked out and get a good one. I like to put vanilla yogurt on my pancakes with just a little bit of maple syrup on top...yum. Makes 10 pancakes.

JERBEAR'S GERMAN POTATO PANCAKES

6 yukon gold potatoes
8 cups water
1 bunch scallion, chopped
1 teaspoon kosher salt
½ teaspoon white pepper

Bring whole unpeeled potatoes to a boil in salted water. Cover and cook until they are tender when pierced with a fork. Drain and let cool slightly. Using a manual grater, shred cooked potato into a large mixing bowl while still warm, being careful not to mash too much. Add scallion, salt, and white pepper, tossing lightly with finger tips as to not mash it up. Season to taste.

Using plastic wrap, pull out an 18-20 inch section of wrap and lay it out on a work surface. Add the potato mixture onto the plastic, forming a log that can be wrapped up in the plastic. After rolling up the mixture, grab up the slack both ends of plastic roll and holding tightly, twist repetitively to squeeze the potatoes into a tight roll. Refrigerate at least 3 hours.

Next, you can cut right through the plastic to form ½ inch cakes, removing plastic pieces before browning. In a hot skillet with minimal oil, brown cakes, about 1 minute per side. You can serve immediately, or brown first and reheat in the oven later. Serve with Buffy apple butter (pg. 141) and sour cream. Makes 12 cakes.

EGGS *with* COLLARD RIBBONS

Greens for breakfast are not very common here in the United States, but greens are so good for us. They are filled with vital non-sugary nutrients, and eating them in the morning feels great.

½ bunch collard greens, washed and chopped into thin ribbons
2 tablespoons + 1 teaspoon water
4 eggs
Sea salt

In a saucepan, add collard greens and water and cover with a lid for 3 minutes. Cook on medium heat. Make little wells in the collards and gently crack one egg in each well. Reduce heat to low. Add 1 teaspoon water and re-cover again (or until the eggs are how you like them). Season with sea salt. Serves 2.

SCRAMBLED EGGS *with* ONIONS, KALE *and* FETA

This dish is quick and easy to make. I try to eat dark leafy greens at least 2 times a day. And the way I see it, if I can get greens into my diet in the morning, it's a good thing (it doesn't matter how).

Olive oil or butter
½ onion, sliced
4 leaves kale, de-stemmed and sliced
1 tablespoon water
4 eggs, cracked and beaten with a fork in a bowl
2 tablespoons feta, crumbled
Sea salt and pepper to taste

In a medium sized saucepan, add 1 teaspoon olive oil or butter. Add onion and sauté on medium heat until translucent. Add kale and sauté for about a minute. Add 1 tablespoon water and cover with a lid until the kale is soft but still bright green, about 2 minutes. Add salt, pepper, and eggs, and scramble over medium heat until the eggs are firm but not dry (stir often). Add feta cheese. Serves 2.

OPTIONS

You can add onion, mushrooms, bacon, leek, carrots, cabbage, tomato and basil. You can substitute tofu for eggs.

SCRAMBLED TOFU *with* SHIITAKE MUSHROOMS *and* ONION

Tofu is like scrambled eggs, in that you can add just about anything you want to it. You do have to season tofu a bit more than eggs, given that tofu has a mild (some say bland) flavor.

1 teaspoon olive oil or sesame oil
½ onion, diced
4 fresh shitake mushrooms or white crimini mushrooms, sliced
½ pound firm tofu, crumbled
1 tablespoon soy sauce
1 teaspoon turmeric
1 tablespoon parsley leaves
Salt and pepper to taste

In a medium sized saucepan, add 1 teaspoon oil. Bring to medium heat. Add onion and sauté until translucent. Add mushrooms and sauté for about 2 minutes, until the mushrooms are soft. Add the tofu, soy sauce, and turmeric, and sauté until well-cooked. If the mixture gets too dry, add a little water. Garnish with parsley, salt and pepper. Serves 2.

OPTIONS

Other great things to add are carrots, cabbage, onions and kale.

SOUPS

ITALIAN WHITE BEAN SOUP

2 cups dry lima or cannellini beans
1 California bay leaf
1 onion, diced
1 carrot, diced or jewel cut
1 stick of celery, diced or jewel cut
3 cloves of garlic, sliced
1 tablespoon dried basil
2 teaspoons dried oregano
Sea salt and pepper
5 cherry tomatoes, halved
Fresh basil and Italian parsley, chopped
Extra-virgin olive oil

Rinse beans and soak in water overnight. Drain beans and discard soaking water. Transfer beans to a pot and add water to cover the beans. Bring to a boil and slow-boil uncovered for 5 minutes. Skim any foam that arises to the top. Add bay leaf. Cover and boil for 45 minutes. After 45 minutes, add onion, carrots, celery, garlic, dried basil and oregano. Boil covered for 30 minutes. (Add water if the water level is getting low. You want just enough water to cover the beans.) When the beans are at their creamy perfection, add sea salt, pepper, tomatoes, parsley, olive oil, and fresh basil as a garnish.

OPTION

Add ½ cup cooked chopped chestnuts to the soup for a great winter flavor.

CHICKEN TORTILLA SOUP

6 corn tortillas
1 tablespoon olive oil
3 tablespoons olive oil
⅛ teaspoon sea salt
1 medium onion, peeled and cut in half (halves left for blackening)
1 red bell pepper, whole, deseeded
2 large cloves garlic, whole
1 jalapeno, whole, deseeded
2 teaspoons chili powder
1 teaspoon chipotle powder
1 (14 oz) can diced tomatoes, drained
2 quarts homemade chicken stock or canned low-sodium chicken broth
2 tablespoons lime juice, plus 1 lime cut into wedges
1 whole boneless and skinless chicken breast (12 ounces) cut in half
2 medium ripe avocados, peeled, pitted, and cut into ½-inch dice
1 ½ cups grated mild white cheddar or Monterey Jack cheese
½ cup packed fresh cilantro leaves

Preheat the oven to 350 degrees. Cut the corn tortillas in half and then crosswise into ⅛-inch-wide strips. Toss in 1 tablespoon olive oil and ⅛ teaspoon sea salt. Put the corn tortilla strips on a baking sheet and bake for 10-15 minutes, until they are just beginning to crisp.

Heat 2 tablespoons oil in a large stockpot over medium heat. Add the onion, red bell pepper, garlic and jalapeno, and cook until they blacken. You will have to pull out the garlic and jalapeno first (they blacken the fastest). Put onion, red bell, garlic, jalapeno, chili powder, chipotle, and garlic in a food processor and blend till smooth.

In the stockpot, on high heat, pour in the can of tomatoes and sear until the color of the tomatoes darken a little. Add onion, garlic, bell pepper, and jalapeno mixture and keep cooking.

In another pot, add the chicken stock and bring to a boil. Reduce the heat to low and add 2 tablespoons lime juice and the chicken. Partially cover and gently simmer until the chicken is no longer pink, about 10-15 minutes.

Use a slotted spoon to remove the chicken from the stock; cool slightly. With your hands, shred the chicken into bite-sized pieces. (The stock and chicken can be refrigerated separately overnight.)

Pour the chicken stock into the tomato mixture. Add the shredded chicken pieces. Add salt, lime and chili powder to taste. Simmer for 10 minutes.

To serve, top each bowl with 1 to 2 tablespoons of cheese, avocado, corn tortillas, and a generous sprinkling of cilantro leaves. Place the remaining cheese and lime wedges on the table for guests to add to their individual bowls as desired. Serves 6-8.

FRENCH LENTIL SOUP

I like lentils because they are quick to cook, you don't have to soak them, and there are so many different cool varieties. French Lentils get creamy and delicious when cooked. In this recipe, I do not sauté the vegetables, because the flavors of the vegetables come out deliciously on their own. I also don't add celery for the simple reason that I don't like celery too much. If you must, feel free to add as much diced celery as you like. Just don't tell me...

1 cup French lentils
5 cups water
1 onion, diced
2 tablespoons olive oil
2 cloves garlic, minced
2 carrots, diced
1 teaspoon dried basil
1 teaspoon dried thyme
1-2 tomatoes, cubed
Sea salt to taste
Fresh chopped parsley for garnish

Put all ingredients in a pot except the salt and tomatoes. Bring to a boil and simmer for 50 minutes, stir occasionally. When the beans are completely soft, add the tomatoes and sea salt. Simmer for 5 minutes. Serve hot with a little olive oil drizzled on the top along with parsley. Serves 4.

OPTION

You can add 2-3 leaves fresh chopped kale or spinach at the end of cooking to give some green to the soup.

WILLO'S THAI RED LENTIL SOUP

Willo was one of my greatest culinary teachers, and she taught me how to make this soup. The thing is, Willo refused to use recipes, and so this soup came out different every time. She would simply pat the side of the pot and say, "It's a good one." In honor of Willo's teaching, I am only going to give you a basic ingredient list for this soup, and I will only offer the principles of how to make it.

For this dish, there is a very important balance of sweet, salty and sour. Thai cooking has lots of sweet added to it, as well as lots of sour. Toasted sesame oil adds great touch to this recipe, and feel free to salt to taste. When I make this soup, I constantly adjust the flavorings to get it right for however I'm feeling at that moment. Willo taught me to use a variety of each type of flavor to make this soup so magnificent and rich. Have fun!

1 cup red lentils
1 -14 oz can coconut milk
2 cups water
1 onion, diced
2 cloves of garlic, minced
2 inches fresh ginger, minced
¼ teaspoon cayenne
2 sprigs cilantro, de-stemmed and chopped
2 sprigs mint, de-stemmed and chopped
2 sprigs basil, de-stemmed and chopped
1 lime, sliced into thin wheels

SOUR OPTIONS

Lemon juice
Lime juice
Rice vinegar

SALT OPTIONS

Soy sauce
Sweet miso*
Sea salt

SWEET OPTIONS

Sugar
Honey
Agave

OIL OPTIONS

Olive oil
Toasted sesame oil

In a pot, put the lentils, coconut milk and water, and bring to a boil. Reduce heat and simmer. Add the onion, ginger, garlic and cayenne. Stir. Do not cover. Once the lentils are cooked and not firm (about 15-20 minutes), add one thing from the sour category, one from the sweet, one from the salty, and some oil (add about a teaspoon oil at a time). Taste. Repeat with a different item from each category. Garnish with sliced wheels of lime and minced up basil, mint, and cilantro. Enjoy! Serves 4.

* Remember with miso, you want to make a paste of miso and water before you add it to the soup. Otherwise the miso will just be a big un-dissolved lump at the bottom of the pot.

COCONUT MUNG DAL

This simple dal tastes great on its own, or as a side with other Indian dishes. Mung beans end up creamy in this recipe, and do not require overnight soaking (unlike many other beans).

1 ½ cups of whole mung beans
2 cups water
1 (14 oz) can of coconut milk
A large knob of ginger, peeled and finely grated (about 2 tablespoons)
6 cloves of garlic, finely chopped or crushed
2 teaspoons garam masala powder
1 yellow onion, diced
1 sweet potato, chopped
1 teaspoon of sea salt
1 lime
¼ bunch cilantro leaves, picked

Pick over the beans very well to look for small stones. Remove any stones. Rinse and drain the beans. In a medium sized pot, add water, beans and the coconut milk. Bring to a boil and reduce to a simmer. After 10 minutes, add the ginger, garlic, garam masala, onion and sweet potato. Bring to a boil. Do not add sea salt at this point.

Turn the heat down to a simmer and partially cover. Simmer 35-45 minutes, stirring and checking the water from time to time. Add more if need be. When the beans are creamy, add sea salt and juice of one lime.

Garnish with cilantro leaves and serve with basmati rice. Serves 4-6.

OPTION

Using split mung beans will cut the cooking time by ⅓.

CURRIED BUTTERNUT COCONUT SOUP *with* PEANUTS

Peanuts with coconut and squash is a delicious combination. I love to serve this with pizza. I know, not exactly Italian, but I like it.

2 tablespoons olive oil
4 cups butternut squash (or sweet potato), peeled and cut into ½-inch dice
2 cups chopped onion
1 tablespoon minced garlic
1 teaspoon curry powder
4 cups water
1 (14 oz) can unsweetened coconut milk
⅓ cup smooth natural peanut butter
½ teaspoon sea salt, or to taste
¼ cup chopped peanuts
Chopped Italian parsley, for garnish

Place oil, squash, onion, garlic, curry, and water into a pot and bring to a boil. Simmer for 20 minutes. Add coconut milk, peanut butter and salt. Purée in the blender until creamy smooth. Garnish with parsley and chopped peanuts. Serves 6-8.

ABOUT BAY LEAVES

I don't keep bay leaves on hand. It drives my chef friends crazy. Every time I get a bay leaf from the store, it's dry, brown, and has no scent or flavor. I might as well buy cardboard. Given that bay leaves are in virtually every soup recipe, I find it odd that Italian bay leaves (Laurus nobilis) from the store add nothing that I can sense. Maybe the chefs in Italy know that fresh leaves from a nearby tree taste good, and they don't think to mention how much freshness matters. But here, where we can only get the stale, desiccated leaves, I don't understand why anyone would want to cook with them.

I do like local California bay leaves (Umbellularia Californica) from trees that grow locally here. The leaves are a different species than the Italian bay tree, and they are edible, flavorful, abundant, potent, fresh, and delicious. Now this is the kind of thing worthy of a soup. Go out and pick them yourself. You only need a small part of leaf to flavor a soup. Still, be careful not to breathe in the leaves too deeply; they are very potent. Which is, of course, what makes them great.

CHESTNUT PUMPKIN SOUP

1 sugar pumpkin or butternut squash, baked until soft
2 onions, chopped
15 cooked chestnuts or 1 cup chestnut puree or 4 tablespoons chestnut flour
2 teaspoons sea salt
½ teaspoon white pepper
Water
2 tablespoons olive oil
4 sprigs fresh thyme

In a pot, place cooked and peeled pumpkin, onions, chestnuts, sea salt, white pepper. Add just enough water to cover the vegetables. Boil for 20 minutes. In a blender, mix soup with olive oil. Drizzle more olive oil on top and garnish with fresh thyme. Serves 6-8.

GINGERED KABOCHA SQUASH SOUP

1 medium large kabocha squash* chopped into 1-inch cubes
1 tablespoon olive oil
1 onion, chopped
2 garlic cloves, minced
2 tablespoons freshly peeled and grated ginger**
1 ½ teaspoon sea salt
¼ teaspoon cumin powder
Water
3 tablespoons fresh lemon juice

In a pot, place cut squash, olive oil, onions, water, garlic, ginger, sea salt, and cumin. Boil for 20 minutes. Pour in just enough water to cover vegetables.

Purée with a hand blender or in a regular blender until creamy smooth. Add lemon and salt to taste.

*By leaving the kabocha peel on, you will make your soup a little greener in color. If you do not want that, peel the squash.

**A great trick for peeling ginger is to use the edge of a regular soup spoon to rub off the peel.

PAZ'S SPANISH CHICKPEA STEW *with* SMOKED PAPRIKA

(POTAJE *de* GARBANZOS *con* PIMENTÓN AHUMADO)

My friend, Paz, first introduced me to this excellent vegetarian soup. It has smoked paprika in it. Smoked paprika is a revelation to me, and there are so many kinds...sweet smoked paprika... hot smoked paprika...there is a whole world of paprika! Who knew? This vegetarian dish has a meaty/savory feel to it, thanks, of course, to the smoked paprika.

1 cup dried chickpeas, soaked overnight in water (or a 2-cup can of cooked chickpeas)
Water
2 garnet or jewel yams, peeled and cubed to ½ inch cubes
2 carrots, diced
1 yellow onion, diced
4 cloves of garlic
1 California bay leaf
2 teaspoons sweet smoked paprika or to taste
½ of a lemon, juiced
Sea salt to taste
Olive oil

Strain the soaked chickpeas, refill with water covering them by 2 inches, and boil for 90 minutes until soft. Add the yams, carrots, onions, bay leaf, salt and garlic (if you need to add more water to keep things covered, do so). Let simmer for 45 minutes. Add smoked paprika. Adjust flavorings. Drizzle with olive oil and lemon juice. Serves 6-8.

OPTION

You can blend up ¼ of the soup to make the broth richer.

CARAMELIZED FRENCH ONION SOUP

6 onions, sliced into half moons
1 teaspoon sea salt
2 teaspoons brown sugar
2 cloves garlic, minced
2 cups finely diced carrot
1 cup diced celery
2 teaspoons fresh thyme
1 teaspoon fresh rosemary, minced
1 California bay leaf
2 quarts vegetable stock, chicken stock or water
2 cups sherry or dry red wine
¼ teaspoon ground pepper
Croutons*
Shredded Parmesan

In a large saucepan over a medium-hot flame, combine the onions, salt, and brown sugar. Continue to cook, stirring occasionally until the onions are very soft and dark caramel brown, about ½ hour. Add the garlic, carrots, celery, thyme, rosemary, and bay leaf. Stir. Add the stock and sherry, cover, and simmer for about 40 minutes. Add pepper and serve with croutons and shredded Parmesan on the side.

If you have time, ladle the soup into a ceramic bowl, cover with croutons and cheese, and bake at 350 degrees for 15 minutes, or until all the cheese melts. Serves 8.

*To make croutons, simply toss cubed sourdough bread with olive oil, sea salt, and pepper. Bake at 350 degrees until almost crispy.

GREENS

SAUTÉED SPRING GREENS IN OLIVE OIL

SPICY ORANGE KALE

BRUSSELS SPROUTS WITH PANCETTA AND GOAT CHEESE

SESAME KALE

RAW KALE SALAD

SAUTÉED CHARD WITH SMOKED CHICKEN

COUVE

BLANCHED BROCCOLI WITH CARROT GINGER DRESSING

COLLARD GREENS WITH PEARS

BASIC BRUSSELS SPOUTS

SAUTÉED SPRING GREENS *in* OLIVE OIL

Mustard greens and dandelions are the very essence of spring, with their delicious bitter flavor. Mustard greens and kale grow all over the farm at RDI. Bitter is one of the 5 tastes our tongue can pick up, and bitter is a flavor that we start to crave if we don't get enough. (There is a reason why coffee, chocolate, and beer are so popular. They are all bitter. While coffee, chocolate and beer have some health benefits, they are not exactly the ideal daily bitters for our bodies...even though I like them...a lot.)

It is essential to have plenty of bitter things in our diet for good digestion and elimination. Whenever I feel sluggish in my brain or body, I go for bitters to restore balance. Try having bitter greens on a daily basis and notice how your body feels.

½ bunch mustard greens
½ bunch kale
½ bunch dandelion
1 tablespoon olive oil
2 cloves minced garlic
1 tablespoon water
Juice of ½ lemon

Wash and chop greens. Heat olive oil, add garlic, and sauté for a few seconds. Add greens and stir for about 1 minute. Add water, reduce heat, and cover until all leaves are wilted, about 5 minutes. Sprinkle the greens with lemon juice. Serves 3-4.

SPICY ORANGE KALE

In Atlanta, Georgia, greens taste good everywhere you go. You may also notice that by every stove, there is bowl with white crystals in it, crystals that look a lot like salt. I learned the hard way what goes in that bowl, when I tried to salt my food and it only made it sweeter. This recipe doesn't have any sugar in it. But if you're in the south, and you reach for the salt, do make sure that it is what you think it is.

1 tablespoon olive oil
1 small onion, thinly sliced
2 garlic cloves, minced
3 bunches kale, washed and sliced to ½ inch thickness
1-inch knob of ginger, peeled and minced
Zest from 1 orange
Juice from 1 orange
2 teaspoons sea salt
½ teaspoon red pepper flakes
½ cup water

In a large skillet, heat up olive oil on medium heat. Sauté the onion and garlic until they begin to brown. Add the kale and ginger and sauté for 2 minutes. Add the zest, orange juice, salt, red pepper flakes and water and cover with a lid. Let steam for 3-5 minutes or until the greens are bright green but tender. Serves 8.

BRUSSELS SPROUTS *with* BALSAMIC VINEGAR, PANCETTA, *and* GOAT CHEESE

2 pounds fresh Brussels sprouts, trimmed and halved
1 tablespoon olive oil
½ teaspoon sea salt
2 garlic cloves, chopped
6 ounces thinly sliced pancetta or cooked bacon, chopped
2 tablespoons balsamic vinegar
¼ cup goat chevre, crumbled

Blanch the Brussels sprouts in lightly salted boiling water for 5-8 minutes, until tender. Pour olive oil in a skillet, and sauté Brussels sprouts, sea salt, and garlic until they start to brown. Add balsamic vinegar and pancetta. Garnish with goat cheese. Serves 6-8.

SESAME KALE

2 cloves garlic, minced
1 bunch kale
2 teaspoons toasted sesame oil
2 tablespoons water
1 teaspoon soy sauce
2 teaspoons toasted sesame seeds
Sea salt and pepper to taste

Mince the garlic cloves.

Wash the kale, and shake it over the sink. It should remain a little wet. Remove and discard the stems from the kale, and tear it into bite-size pieces. You can chop up the stems finely and sauté separately if you like.

Heat the sesame oil in the skillet over medium-low heat. Add the minced garlic to the hot oil and sauté for about 20 seconds. Add the kale and water to the garlic and oil, and cover the skillet. After 1 minute, stir the kale, then re-cover. After 1-2 more minutes, when the kale is wilted, stir in the soy sauce and sesame seeds. If desired, add salt and/or pepper to taste. Serves 3-4.

RAW KALE SALAD

1 bunch kale
2 tablespoons olive oil
1 tablespoon sea salt
1 lemon, juiced
1 tablespoon agave or honey
½ cup pumpkin seeds
5 radishes chopped
1 avocado, diced

Chop the kale into 1-inch pieces and put in a large bowl. Add oil, salt, lemon juice, and agave, and massage for about 5 minutes until the kale looks softer and more broken down. Add the other ingredients and enjoy. I like to prepare this dish an hour or two before serving, minus the avocado. Just before serving add the avocado. Serves 4.

OPTIONS

You can use any dark leafy greens, dried or fresh fruit, and/or nuts or seeds to make variations on this delicious salad.

SAUTÉED CHARD *with* SMOKED CHICKEN

I taught cooking at the Excelsior School in the outer mission neighborhood of San Francisco. I worked through Project Ole, a garden and cooking school program. The students were a very diverse group of kids, and many were used to a fast-food diet. Getting them to eat their vegetables wasn't as hard as I thought. I learned that if I added smoked chicken or some kind of meat to the greens, the kids would go for them. This was especially cool since they were growing the vegetables themselves in their schoolyard.

1 onion, sliced into half moons
2 cloves garlic, minced
1 tablespoon olive oil
½ teaspoon sea salt
1 bunch chard washed, de-stemmed and sliced
¼ pound smoked shredded chicken

On medium heat, sauté the onion, garlic, and salt in olive oil. Add the chard and chicken, and cook until the chard is soft, about 4 minutes. Serves 4.

OPTION

Add 2 strips of cooked and diced bacon instead of the smoked chicken.

COUVE (BRAZILIAN GARLIC COLLARDS)

I like to find any way to get dark leafy greens into my body, and this Brazilian way to make greens is a great one. I like to serve this with moquekah (pg. 114).

2 bunches collard greens, washed
1 tablespoon olive oil
1 teaspoon sea salt
4 cloves garlic, minced
2 tablespoons water

Stack the collard greens and roll them into a giant cigar shape. Slice the collards into as thin ribbons as you can manage. Super wafer thin! In a skillet, heat up the olive oil. Add the greens, garlic, salt and sauté for 3 minutes. Add water and cover with a lid for 3 minutes or so, until the collards are bright green. Adjust salt to taste.

OPTION

You can add chopped, cooked bacon to this dish as well.

BLANCHED BROCCOLI *with* CARROT GINGER DILL DRESSING

I love this dressing because it has so many raw and fresh ingredients. You can serve this on top of blanched greens or on a hearty green salad.

1 bunch broccoli, blanched or steamed

1 tablespoon diced onion
1 cup grated carrots
2 teaspoons peeled and minced ginger, or 2 teaspoons powdered ginger
1 teaspoon mustard
2 teaspoons finely chopped fresh dill, or 1 tablespoon dried dill
2 tablespoons soy sauce
2 tablespoons apple cider or apple juice
4 tablespoons apple cider vinegar
6 tablespoons olive oil
1 teaspoon toasted sesame oil

To blanch the broccoli: boil a pot of water with a pinch of sea salt in about 2 inches of water. Add the broccoli and cook for 2-3 minutes until bright green. Remove from hot water and let cool on a cutting board.

Mix all of the ingredients (except the broccoli) in a blender and puree until smooth. Pour on top of your broccoli or green salad. Serves 3-4.

COLLARD GREENS *with* PEARS, BALSAMIC VINEGAR *and* TOASTED PECANS

I learned how to cook collards this way in Atlanta, Georgia. This is one of my favorite ways to make them.

¼ cup pecans, toasted then chopped
2 teaspoons olive oil
1 bunch of collards, washed and cut into ribbons
1 pear, sliced
1 tablespoon balsamic vinegar
Water
Sea salt to taste

Place pecans on a baking sheet and bake for 8 minutes at 350 degrees, or until you can smell their fragrance. Let cool and chop.

In a skillet, pour 2 teaspoons olive oil. Heat on medium heat. Place collards, balsamic vinegar, and pears in the pan. Stir. Add 1 tablespoon of water and a pinch of sea salt. Cover for about 3 minutes. Check to see if the collards are done to your liking. Add water (if needed) to keep greens from burning. Add pecans and serve. Serves 3–4.

OPTION

You can substitute apples for pears in this recipe.

BASIC BRUSSELS SPROUTS

2 pounds Brussels sprouts, stemmed and halved
1 teaspoon sea salt
2 tablespoons olive oil
3 tablespoons water

Preheat oven to 400 degrees. In a bowl, toss Brussels sprouts in sea salt, olive oil, and water. Place cut side down in a baking pan. Cover with foil and bake. After 20 minutes, remove foil and cook for 10 minutes to brown the Brussels sprouts. Serves 4-6.

BAKED YAMS WITH GINGER HONEY BUTTER AND CRANBERRIES

DELICATTA BOATS

KINPURA

CURRIED ROASTED CAULIFLOWER WITH RAISINS AND ALMONDS

MARINATED BEET SALAD WITH MINT

YUKON GOLD AND GARNET YAM GRATIN

MASHED POTATOES WITH PARSNIP,
CARAMELIZED ONIONS, AND BLUE CHEESE

MOROCCAN CARROT SALAD

SCAPES

ROASTED BEETS WITH GOAT CHEESE

BAKED YAMS *with* GINGER HONEY BUTTER *and* CRANBERRIES

Eating sweet vegetables satisfies my sugar cravings, and they are much healthier than other sweet options. I try to have a sweet vegetable at every meal I serve. This method to make baked yams is easy and brings out the best in the yams. I eat these plain, with butter, or with ginger honey butter drizzle.

THE YAMS

3 garnet or jewel yams
2 tablespoons olive oil
1 teaspoon sea salt

Preheat oven to 400 degrees. Wash the yams. Coat the yams in olive oil and sea salt. Do not poke holes into the yams. The intact skin of the yam allows it to steam itself. Place on a baking sheet and cook for 45 minutes to 1 hour, until soft. Remove from oven and cut into thirds.

GINGER HONEY BUTTER DRIZZLE

4 tablespoons butter
1 tablespoon fresh grated ginger
1 tablespoon honey
Pinch of sea salt
2 tablespoons dried cranberries

In a saucepan, melt the butter with the ginger. Let simmer for about 2 minutes. Add the honey and sea salt. Pour over the baked yams and garnish with dried cranberries. Serves 4-6.

DELICATTA BOATS *with* WEHANI RED RICE, CRANBERRIES, *and* SAGE

Delicatta is one of the more delicious of the squashes, and you can eat it with the skin on!

2 delicatta squash
1 tablespoon butter
½ medium yellow onion, finely chopped
1 garlic clove, minced
2 teaspoons chopped fresh sage or ½ teaspoon dried
2 tablespoons chopped walnuts
½ apple, small dice
½ cup cooked wehani (red) rice or brown rice
1 tablespoon dried cranberries
2 tablespoons freshly shredded Parmesan cheese

Preheat oven to 350 degrees. Slice the delicatta lengthwise and scoop out the seeds with a spoon. Oil the seeded delicatta and place face down on a cookie sheet. Bake for 20-30 minutes until the squash feels done but is still firm (do not over-cook at this stage).

Melt the butter in a large frying pan over medium-high heat. Add onions, garlic, and salt. Cook, stirring occasionally, until onions are soft, about 3 minutes. Stir in sage and cook until fragrant, about 1 minute. Stir in nuts, apple, rice, and cranberries. Set aside.

Portion out the rice stuffing among squash halves, put it in the cut side of the squash, sprinkle with Parmesan, and bake until the tops are just beginning to brown and squash is tender when pierced with a fork, about 25 minutes. Serves 4.

OPTION

You can add ¼ pound cooked ground turkey to the dish for your carnivorous friends.

KINPURA

Kinpura is a dish whose name means "sauté and simmer" in Japanese. I love this dish because when I eat it, I feel centered. Burdock is a medicinal root, thought to strengthen the blood, and seaweed is high in minerals as well.

I learned about this dish when I was studying macrobiotics and the effect food can have on our mood. Macrobiotics teaches that in order create peace in ourselves and in the world, the first thing we do is start with our diet. I like to eat this with brown rice, blanched kale, and miso lemon tahini sauce (pg. 87).

2 teaspoons olive oil
1 cup matchsticked burdock root*
1 teaspoon sea salt
1 cup matchsticked parsnip
1 cup matchsticked carrot
1 cup matchsticked daikon
¼ cup soaked arame seaweed
2 tablespoons water
1 teaspoon dark or light sesame oil
Soy sauce
2 tablespoons toasted pumpkin seeds

Heat olive oil in a heavy skillet over medium heat. Add burdock and sea salt. Stir until coated with oil, about 2 minutes. Add carrots and parsnips. Stir for 2 more minutes. Add daikon. Stir for 2 minutes. Add seaweed and water. Cover and cook over medium-low heat about 10 minutes. Season lightly with soy sauce and sesame oil, and simmer until any liquid that remains has been absorbed (about 10 minutes). Stir well before transferring to a serving platter. Garnish with toasted pumpkin seeds. Serves 6–8.

*Matchsticking is a style of cutting vegetables so that they are as thin as matchsticks.

CURRIED ROASTED CAULIFLOWER *with* GOLDEN RAISINS *and* ALMONDS

2 heads cauliflower, cores removed, cut into florets
2-4 tablespoons olive oil
1 teaspoon sea salt
½ teaspoon fine ground black pepper
2 teaspoons Indian curry powder
½ cup golden raisins, soaked in water for 20 minutes
⅓ cup rough chopped almonds, toasted

Preheat the oven to 400 degrees. Toss cauliflower with the olive oil first, then sprinkle on sea salt, pepper and curry powder, and toss again. Place cauliflower on a baking sheet and roast for 20 minutes or until browned.

Transfer cauliflower to a bowl, and toss in the raisins and toasted almonds. Serve warm or at room temperature. Adjust sea salt. Serves 6.

MARINATED BEET SALAD *with* MINT

1 pound beets
3 tablespoons balsamic vinegar
3/4 cup orange juice
¼ bunch fresh mint, leaves picked and chopped

Bring water to boil. Add beets and let cook for 45 minutes or until soft. When beets are done, run under cold water and remove the skins.

Once beets are cooled, slice into ¼ moons. Toss with balsamic vinegar and orange juice. Dress with fresh mint. You can eat this right away, or let marinate over night. It gets better the longer it sits.

OPTIONS

Feel free to add goat cheese or feta to this. Finely sliced fennel is also nice in this, as are toasted walnuts.

YUKON GOLD POTATO *and* GARNET YAM GRATIN *with* GRUYERE

Gratin means cheesy, dreamy, creamy vegetables. This is a decadent dish, and very forgiving to make. But be forewarned, when I make this recipe, I find myself eating the scrapings at the bottom of the pan.

1 pound yukon gold potatoes, sliced into thin slices (leave the peel on)
½ pound garnet yams, sliced into thin slices (peel on)
1 teaspoon olive oil
1 teaspoon sea salt
½ teaspoon black pepper
½ teaspoon nutmeg (nutmeg is essential)
1 cup grated gruyere or swiss cheese
8 tablespoons shredded Parmesan cheese
⅔ cup heavy cream

Preheat oven to 400 degrees. Oil a 8x10 sized glass baking pan. In a bowl, mix the salt, pepper, nutmeg, and cream with the yams and potatoes. Place half of the potato and yam mixture in the bottom of the pan. Cover with ½ of the gruyere and Parmesan. Place the remaining potato and yam mixture on top, then place the remaining cheese on top of that, ending with Parmesan. Bake covered for 40-50 minutes. Check to make sure the potatoes are soft and the cream is thickening up. Remove the cover, and let cheese brown for 10 minutes. Serves 4.

OPTIONS

You can add all kinds of things to this recipe: truffle oil, sautéed onions, goat cheese, bacon, and blue cheese.

MASHED POTATOES *with* PARSNIP, CARAMELIZED ONIONS, *and* BLUE CHEESE

Mashers with parsnips are a great seasonal combination. Add onions and blue cheese, and you have a wonderful side dish.

1 tablespoon olive oil
3 yellow onions, sliced into half moons
1 tablespoon brown sugar
Water
½ teaspoon sea salt
4 yukon gold potatoes, cubed
6 parsnips, cut into 1-inch chunks
1 cup vegetarian broth, warmed
¼ cup blue cheese, crumbled
3 tablespoons fresh thyme, chopped
Sea salt and pepper to taste

Heat oil in a large skillet. Cook onions with the sugar until the onions brown, about 20 minutes. Fill a stockpot with water and sea salt; bring to a boil. Add potatoes and parsnips and bring to a boil. Reduce to a simmer until the potatoes and parsnips are tender but not mushy. Drain. Mix the potato/parsnip mixture and broth with a masher or in food processor. Fold in the onions, blue cheese and thyme. Salt and pepper to taste. Serves 8.

MOROCCAN CARROT SALAD

This simple raw salad is refreshing and delicious. I like to serve this with chicken tagine (pg. 113) and Israeli couscous (pg. 131).

2 carrots, shredded
1 tablespoon raisins
¼ teaspoon ginger powder
¼ teaspoon cinnamon powder
¼ teaspoon allspice powder
2 teaspoons lemon juice
1 teaspoon olive oil
½ teaspoon sea salt

Mix all the ingredients and adjust flavors to taste.

SCAPES

If you are lucky enough to have a garden where you grow garlic, or you get to the farmers market at the right time of year just before the garlic flowers, you might get to buy scapes. At the RDI farm, there are rows and rows of these yummy treats. Scapes are the shoot of the garlic flower, before it flowers. Roasted, they taste like creamy roasted garlic sticks that you can eat like chips. Very delicious.

10 scapes
1 tablespoon olive oil
½ teaspoon sea salt

Preheat oven to 375 degrees. Toss the scapes and place on a baking sheet. Bake for 20 minutes, or until brown. Let cool.

ROASTED BEETS *with* GOAT CHEESE

Borage flowers, besides making a colorful garnish, are a great way to attract bees to your garden.

1 pound beets, medium sized
1 tablespoon olive oil
1 teaspoon sea salt
¼ pound goat chevre
Zest from one orange
Juice from one orange
2 tablespoons balsamic vinegar
Borage or rosemary flowers (optional)

Preheat oven to 400 degrees. Leaving the skin on, cut the beets in thick wedges (like you would a potato home fry). Toss the beets in olive oil and sea salt. Put on a baking pan and bake for 45 minutes to 60 minutes, until the beets are soft.

In a bowl, toss the cooked beets with orange zest, juice and balsamic vinegar. Place on a serving plate, and gently put small clumps of goat chevre all over the top of the beets. Garnish with borage or rosemary flowers for a beautiful blue contrast on the beets. If you don't have the flowers, parsley or mint are also great garnishes for this dish.

CHICKEN SALAD WITH CRISPY RICE NOODLES AND 5 SPICE

GREEN SALAD WITH ROASTED DELICATTA SQUASH,
SPICED PUMPKIN SEEDS AND POMEGRANATE VINAIGRETTE

PERUVIAN SALAD WITH GARLIC AVOCADO DRESSING

BUTTER LETTUCE WITH JICAMA AND PECANS

MISO LEMON TAHINI DRESSING

GARDEN GREENS AND BLUEBERRIES
WITH BLUE CHEESE TARRAGON DRESSING

FATTUSH

GREEN SALAD WITH CARDAMOM CASHEWS
AND LEMON ROSE VINAIGRETTE

ARUGULA SALAD WITH GRAPES, FENNEL,
GORGONZOLA AND PECANS

SALAD WITH PERSIMMONS, DRIED CHERRIES,
WALNUTS AND GOAT CHEVRE

CHICKEN SALAD *with* CRISPY RICE NOODLES *and* FIVE SPICE

This recipe is light and refreshing. It has a lot of steps to it, but they are all easy. Five Spice powder, toasted sesame oil and mustard powder are the base of the flavorings. Five spice commonly has pepper, star anise, fennel, clove, and cinnamon in it. Make sure your mustard powder is fresh to give the right amount of POW in the dressing. Warning: mustard powder is not the same as mustard you put on your hot dog.

You can easily substitute tofu for the chicken to make a vegetarian option. Most of these ingredients are found in your local Asian market or health food store. Rice sticks do not look like sticks in the package. Read the package to make sure the sticks are the fry kind. They look more like thin noodles, sometimes in the shape of a bird nest. This is great for a crowd as it is exciting, easy to make vegetarian/vegan, and it is already gluten free.

MARINADE

2 tablespoons Five spice powder
1 teaspoon minced ginger
1 teaspoon minced garlic
3 tablespoons wheat-free tamari
3 tablespoons white wine (optional)

SALAD TOPPINGS

1 pound boneless skinless chicken thighs
2 heads thinly chopped romaine lettuce
½ package rice sticks (3.5 oz.)
4 cups rice oil or sunflower oil
4 scallions, slivered
¾ cups finely chopped toasted peanuts, almonds or cashews
3 tablespoons toasted brown or black sesame seeds
Cilantro for garnish

SALAD DRESSING

½ cup honey or agave
1 tablespoon sea salt
1 teaspoon black pepper
1 ¼ cup light olive oil, rice oil, or sunflower oil
¼ cup toasted sesame oil
1 cup rice wine vinegar
1 ½ teaspoon dry mustard powder

In a bowl, put the marinade in with the chicken. Make sure it is all coated. Let the chicken sit in the fridge ideally overnight (however, if you didn't think that far ahead, just coat the meat for 5 minutes). Preheat the oven to 375 degrees and cook the marinated thighs for 20-30 minutes. Let cool, slice into strips.

Mix all the dressing ingredients in a blender.

In a pot, put 4 cups of oil and heat on the stove. Break the rice sticks in half. Place the sticks in the hot oil. They will puff immediately. Remove immediately and place on a paper towel or brown paper bag. Repeat. (After you are done you can strain the oil and save it for future frying).

In a bowl, toss the lettuce with ⅔ of the dressing. In another, toss the chicken and nuts with the remaining ⅓ of the dressing.

Place the lettuce in a serving bowl. Put a nest of noodles on top, then dressed chicken and nuts. Sprinkle sesame seeds along the edge of the lettuce and garnish with scallions and cilantro.

GREEN SALAD *with* ROASTED DELICATTA SQUASH, GOAT CHEESE, SPICED PUMPKIN SEEDS, *and* POMEGRANATE VINAIGRETTE

I adapted this from a recipe given to me by Amy Murray, owner of Venus Restaurant in Berkeley, California. You can get pomegranate molasses at most health food stores.

SALAD

1 delicatta squash
2 teaspoons olive oil
½ teaspoon sea salt
¼ teaspoon black pepper
¼ pomegranate, de-seeded
¼ cup goat cheese, crumbled
1 bunch green leaf lettuce, washed, chopped and dried

Slice the delicatta into rounds (full moon shapes) about ¼ inch thick. Spoon out the seeds. Toss in olive oil, salt and pepper and roast at 350 degrees for 30 minutes, or until browned and soft. Let cool. Toss the greens in the pomegranate vinaigrette. Garnish the salad with roasted delicatta, pumpkin seeds, goat cheese, and pomegranate seeds. Serves 4.

POMEGRANATE VINAIGRETTE

¼ cup pomegranate molasses
¼ cup sherry vinegar
1 teaspoon mustard
1 orange zested and juiced
1 ½ cups olive oil

In a blender, place all ingredients except the oil. Put the blender on low, and slowly pour in the oil. Add salt and pepper to taste.

SPICED PUMPKIN SEEDS

2 tablespoons maple syrup
2 teaspoons powdered cumin
¼ teaspoon cayenne
½ teaspoons sea salt
1 cup pumpkin seeds

Whisk together maple syrup, cumin, cayenne and sea salt. Toss pumpkin seeds with maple syrup mixture. Toast in 350 degree oven for 8-10 minutes.

PERUVIAN SALAD *with* GARLIC AVOCADO DRESSING

When I visited Cuzco, Peru, I had my first introduction to the true magnificence of the potato. In Peru, there are over 1000 different varieties of the potato, each perfectly cultivated for very specific conditions. Potatoes are in everything in multiple ways.

This is a delicious and unusual salad that goes well with the Peruvian chicken (pg. 96), quinoa (pg. 130), and aji amarillo sauce (pg. 137).

SALAD

1 head green leaf lettuce
½ cup rice or sunflower oil
2 yellow finn potatoes, sliced thin into matchsticks
2 roasted beets, peeled
1 ripe avocado
2 hard boiled eggs, peeled
8 kalamata olives

AVOCADO DRESSING

1 avocado
1 clove garlic
2 tablespoons lemon
1 teaspoon sea salt
1 teaspoon honey or sugar
½ cup olive oil

To make the salad, wash and prepare the lettuce. Heat oil in a skillet. Fry the potatoes in the oil until crispy. Put the potatoes on a paper towel to drain. Lightly salt. Slice the beets into chunks. Slice the avocado into chunks. Slice the eggs.

To make the dressing, blend the avocado, garlic, lemon, honey, and sea salt in a blender. While blending, slowly add the olive oil. Adjust seasonings.

Toss the salad with the dressing. Garnish with potatoes, beets, avocados, egg and olives. Serves 4.

BUTTER LETTUCE *with* JICAMA, PECANS, *and* MAPLE DIJON DRESSING

SALAD

1 head of butter lettuce, washed and chopped
¼ cup jicama, peeled and sliced finely
¼ cup pecans, toasted and chopped

MAPLE DIJON DRESSING

1 tablespoon dijon mustard
½ cup balsamic vinegar
¼ cup maple syrup
Salt and pepper to taste
1 cup olive oil

Blend first four ingredients with a wire whisk or food processor. Add oil slowly to emulsify. Adjust to taste. Toss the greens with the dressing, pecans, and jicama. Serves 4.

MISO LEMON TAHINI DRESSING

Great on greens like blanched kale or broccoli!

⅓ cup tahini
1 tablespoon mellow or chickpea miso
1 tablespoon lemon juice
⅓ cup water

Place all the ingredients in a blender and blend until smooth. Adjust ingredients to your taste and consistency. Makes 3/4 cup.

OPTION

You can substitute in orange for lemon, or add 2 tablespoons of poppy seeds to make a nice variation on this classic sauce.

GARDEN GREENS *and* BLUEBERRIES *with* BLUE CHEESE TARRAGON DRESSING

I like to use all kinds of mixed spring greens found on the farm in this salad: arugula, nasturtium leaves, spinach, lemon balm, mustard greens, as well as classic lettuce. The blueberries and tarragon are a great combination, and they add a lot to the flavors of this salad.

DRESSING

2 tablespoons blue cheese
¼ cup blueberries
1 clove minced garlic
⅓ cup unseasoned rice, champagne, or white vinegar
1 teaspoon honey
2 tablespoons minced onion
1 tablespoon fresh tarragon
½ cup olive oil
Salt and pepper to taste

SALAD

4 cups mixed greens
3/4 cup blueberries for garnish
4 nasturtium flowers (optional)

In a blender on low speed, mix the blue cheese, blueberries, garlic, vinegar, honey, onion, and tarragon. Slowly add the oil. Season with salt and pepper to taste. Toss greens with salad and garnish with blueberries and nasturtium flowers. Serves 4.

FATTOUSH

This is a delicious Middle Eastern bread salad. The crispy-ness of the fried pita bread makes this a lively, fun salad.

CRISPY PITA

3 rounds pita bread
2-4 tablespoons rice or sunflower oil
1 teaspoon sea salt

SALAD

4 leaves romaine lettuce, shredded
½ cup scallions, coarsely chopped
1 cup cucumbers, coarsely chopped
2 cups tomatoes, coarsely chopped
1 bunch fresh mint leaves, chopped
1 bunch fresh parsley, chopped
2 cloves garlic, crushed

DRESSING

½ cup lemon juice
⅔ cup olive oil
2 ½ teaspoons sea salt
½ teaspoon sumac (optional)

Tear the pita into small pieces, about 1-inch square. Fry the pita pieces in 2-4 tablespoons of oil, and place them on an absorbent paper towel to drain away the excess oil. Sprinkle the fried pita with sea salt. Note: the pita pieces may be toasted if preferred.

In a large mixing bowl, mix the chopped vegetables and herbs. Add the fried pita bread. In a blender prepare the dressing of lemon juice, oil, garlic, and seasoning, and pour it over the mixture. Correct the seasoning adding more lemon juice if required. Toss and serve in a large salad bowl. Serves 4–6.

OPTION

You can substitute gluten free bread in this recipe.

GREEN SALAD *with* CARDAMOM CASHEWS *and* LEMON ROSE VINAIGRETTE

SALAD

1 head lettuce (red, green or butter) washed and chopped
1 tangerine, peeled and separated into wedges
½ bunch mint, leaves picked off the stems
Cardamom Cashews
Rose Vinaigrette
Fresh rose petals (optional)

Toss the lettuce with the tangerine, mint, cashews and rose vinaigrette. Garnish with fresh rose petals and serve. Serves 4.

CARDAMOM CASHEWS

½ cup cashews
¼ cup sugar
1 tablespoon water
1 teaspoon cardamom powder
⅛ teaspoon cayenne powder

Preheat oven to 350 degrees. Line a baking sheet with parchment paper. Place the sugar, water, cardamom and cayenne into a saucepan. Melt the sugar over medium heat. Add the cashews, and stir until well coated, then spread onto the prepared baking sheet. Bake at 350 degrees for 9 minutes. Remove from parchment immediately and cool to room temperature.

ROSE VINAIGRETTE

½ cup freshly squeezed lemon juice
1 teaspoon Dijon mustard
2 teaspoons rose water
Sea Salt to taste
Dash of pepper
½ cup olive oil

Combine all of the ingredients in a jar and mix thoroughly.

If made ahead, cover and refrigerate, but bring to room temperature and mix again before adding to a salad. Makes 2 cups.

ARUGULA SALAD *with* GRAPES, FENNEL, GORGONZOLA, *and* PECANS

DRESSING

4 teaspoons apricot jam
3 tablespoons white wine vinegar
3 tablespoons olive oil
1 small shallot, minced very fine
Sea salt and ground black pepper

SALAD

½ small fennel bulb, cored, trimmed of stalks, and sliced very thin
2 fennel fronds chopped coarse (from the top of your fennel bulbs)
8 cups lightly packed baby arugula
1 cup red seedless grapes, halved lengthwise
3 oz gorgonzola cheese, crumbled (3/4 cup)
½ cup chopped pecans, toasted

Whisk jam, vinegar, oil, shallot, ¼ teaspoon salt, and ¼ teaspoon pepper in large bowl. Toss fennel with vinaigrette, and let stand 15 minutes. Add arugula, fennel fronds, and grapes, toss and adjust seasonings with salt and pepper.

Divide salad among individual plates, top each with a portion of gorgonzola and pecans. Serve right away. Serves 4–6.

OPTION

You can substitute feta for gorgonzola cheese.

SALAD *with* PERSIMMONS, DRIED CHERRIES, WALNUTS, *and* GOAT CHEVRE

My favorite time of year is when the persimmons are in season. For this recipe, get the fuyu persimmons. They're the hard persimmons that you eat like an apple. This, combined with goat chevre made fresh on the farm, is delicious.

DRESSING

2 teaspoons honey
3 tablespoons red wine vinegar
½ cup dried cherries or cranberries
3 tablespoons olive oil
Sea salt and black pepper to taste

SALAD

1 fuyu persimmon, sliced (if not in season, use apple instead)
¼ pound pre-washed baby greens
½ cup chopped walnuts, toasted
½ cup goat chevre

Whisk honey and vinegar in small saucepan, stir in cherries. Put on the stove and simmer for 5 minutes. Whisk in oil. Add sea salt and pepper to taste. While the mixture is still warm, toss in dried cherries. Let cool to room temperature.

Toss lettuce and cherry mixture in large bowl. Adjust seasonings with salt and pepper. Divide salad among individual plates. Top each salad with a portion of nuts, persimmon, and dollops of goat chevre. Serve immediately. Serves 4.

MAIN DISHES

PERUVIAN ROAST CHICKEN WITH LIME

BAKED ZITI

RAINBOW CHARD AND FETA PIE

MOLE ENCHILADAS WITH CHICKEN

THAI BUTTERNUT SQUASH CURRY

CHICKEN STYLE TOFU

BAKED BEANS

FALAFEL

PIZZA NIGHT

CHICKEN TANDOORI

PUTATOUIE

TINGA TURKEY WITH FETA

BAKED SALMON

CHICKEN TAGINE

MOQUEKA

PAELLA WITH MUSSELS, CLAMS AND ARTICHOKE HEARTS

PERUVIAN ROAST CHICKEN *with* LIME

MARINADE

3 tablespoons olive oil
¼ cup fresh mint leaves
1 tablespoon + 1 ½ teaspoon sea salt
6 garlic cloves
1 tablespoon black pepper
1 tablespoon cumin, ground
1 tablespoon sugar
1 tablespoon smoked paprika
2 teaspoons dried oregano
2 teaspoons lime zest
¼ cup lime juice
1 teaspoon minced jalapeno
4 pounds chicken legs, breasts and thighs

In a blender, mix all the ingredients, except the chicken. Spread the paste over the chicken. Cover and let marinate in the fridge for 6-24 hours.

Preheat the oven to 350 degrees.

Lift chicken out of marinade. Roast on a baking sheet for 30-50 minutes until nice and brown, or until the breast reads at 165 degrees (cooking time varies depending on whether you cook breasts or thighs).

BAKED ZITI

This is chef Nora Vitaliani's ziti recipe. I first had Baked Ziti in New York City at the Beatrice Café on 12th street in the West Village. I would sometimes visit Chef Bruno, who had worked there for 30 years. I had my first real Ziti at the Beatrice Café, and it was creamy and delicious. Baked Ziti is forever in my heart.

1 pound ziti or penne noodles
1 pound ricotta
1 pound mozzarella, shredded
4 cups marinara sauce

Cook the noodles to just al dente as they will continue to cook in the sauce. Mix the noodles with sauce, ricotta, and ¾ of the mozzarella. Spread into a 9x13 baking pan. Sprinkle remaining mozzarella over the top. Bake until golden brown and bubbly. Serves 8-10.

MARINARA

2 -28 oz cans diced tomatoes
5 cloves garlic, crushed
2 tablespoons olive oil
½ teaspoon chili flakes
½ teaspoon fennel seeds
1 teaspoon dried basil
1 teaspoon dried oregano
2 cups water
1 sprig of rosemary
1 bunch of basil leaves, chopped

Heat oil in a heavy bottomed pot. Sauté garlic until translucent, add dried herbs, stir to combine. Add tomatoes, water, and rosemary. Simmer for 2 hours, stirring occasionally. Remove from heat, stir in fresh basil.

OPTION

You can add sausage, ground beef, or vegan sausage/seitan for added protein.

RAINBOW CHARD *and* FETA PIE

The garden at RDI grows the most beautiful chard and garlic. Add fresh goat feta, and newly laid eggs, and we have a delicious farm pie.

1 tablespoon + 1 teaspoon olive oil
1 bunch chard, washed and chopped, stems included (about 8 cups)
2 teaspoons sea salt
1 onion, diced
2 cloves garlic, minced
3 eggs
¾ cup crumbled feta
½ teaspoon allspice powder
20 sheets phylo dough
½ cup salted butter

In a skillet, pour in 1 teaspoon olive oil. Sauté chard and stems with 1 teaspoon sea salt for 5 minutes, stirring constantly. Remove from pan and let cool. After it cools, squeeze out any liquid in the chard with your hands.

In the same skillet, pour in 1 tablespoon olive oil. Sauté onion and garlic with 1 teaspoon sea salt on medium heat until browned. Let cool.

In a bowl, add the chard and cooled onion mixture. Add eggs, feta, and allspice powder. Mix well.

Preheat oven to 350 degrees. In a 8x10 baking pan, grease the bottom of the pan with butter, using a pastry brush. Pull out 2 sheets of phylo and place in pan. If the phylo is bigger than your pan, trim all the phylo with scissors until it fits. Butter the top. Place another 2 sheets, butter. Continue until you have 5 layers of 2 sheets of phylo.

Pour in chard mixture and spread evenly over the phylo. Working quickly, layer phylo 2 sheets at a time, then butter. After layer 4, butter the top. Add one more sheet (not layer), and butter the top of that. Add another sheet and do the same. (This prevents "fly away" phylo when you cook it. The butter helps the phylo stick to itself).

Using your knife, cut off any excess phylo that is hanging over the edge of the pan. Press in the edges with a spatula. Using a knife, cut the phylo into 8 squares (it is much easier to cut phylo before it is cooked). Bake for 45 minutes until golden brown on the top. Serves 6-8.

< Photo on opposite page
Chard is such an amazing survival plant. Penny refers to it as one of our hardy "climate change" plants. It can withstand many climatic conditions. Chard adapts well to sun, shade, drought, coastal, inland, temperate, or subtropical conditions.

MOLE ENCHILADAS *with* CHICKEN

The first time I landed in Mexico, I had no idea where I was going. I had the name of a town on a slip of paper. An hour and a half after having arrived in Mexico, I got off a bus in Tepotzlan, the city on my slip of paper. At the back of the bus was a man, dressed all in white. He was the only other person on the bus with a backpack. When we got off the bus, we struck up a conversation. He was returning from England studying to be a cellist and was going into the jungle to build what he called a Temple of Life.

He then asked if I would care to join him. I said yes, of course, and I remember how alive I felt and how crazy I was to be waking into the jungle with a perfect stranger. In the jungle, we met a family that was building a stone wall in the middle of nowhere. It was there, in the middle of nowhere, that I spent the next 5 days, eating the juice from sugar cane, and bathing in a pool surrounded by very old trees (which I later learned was La Posa de Amatlan, or the birthplace of the plumed serpent diety Quetzalcoatl).

The family building the stone wall had chickens. One day I returned to them, and didn't notice any chickens, but saw a pile of feathers and a whole heap of chicken tamales. There is nothing more delicious than chicken tamales in the jungle.

In Tepotzlan, there was a great outdoor market, and they sold blue corn tacos with goat ricotta and fried crickets. The people at that market also gave me my first real introduction to mole. I was in Tepotzlan around the time of Dias De Los Muertos, and never had I seen a food so appreciated and revered as the mole. From that day on, I've had the mole fever, and whenever I get a chance to have real mole, I jump at it.

This recipe is a bit simpler than your traditional mole, but gives me the satisfaction of real mole and a vivid memory of Tepotzlan.

6 dried ancho chilies
1 cup water
2 tablespoons almonds
2 tablespoons pumpkin seeds
1 tablespoon sesame seeds
2 tablespoons olive oil
1 onion, chopped
1 teaspoon sea salt
4 cloves garlic, minced
1 teaspoon cinnamon
1 teaspoon ground cumin
¼ teaspoon cloves

1 tablespoon molasses
1-14 oz can chopped tomatoes
2 tablespoons cocoa powder, sifted
1 red bell pepper, julienned

1 onion, sliced into half moons
2 cups cooked shredded chicken
2 teaspoons chili powder
1 teaspoon sea salt
12 corn tortillas
½ pound shredded jack cheese

Remove stems from chilies. Combine chilies and water in a saucepan, and bring to a boil. Cover and let stand. Set aside. Combine almonds and pumpkin seeds in a skillet over medium heat. Toast for 2 minutes. Add sesame seeds until lightly browned, stirring frequently. Remove from skillet, set aside to cool.

In a medium skillet, add 1 tablespoon oil, onion, sea salt and garlic. Sauté for 5 minutes. Add cinnamon, cumin and cloves and cook for 1 minute, stirring. Add tomatoes, chilies, molasses, and chocolate. Simmer for 5 minutes.

In a food processor or blender, grind up the nuts and seeds. Add the tomato mixture. Add water to make the mixture medium-thin, like runny ketchup. Pour into a bowl and set aside.

In a skillet, pour 1 tablespoon olive oil and bring to medium heat. Sauté the onions and the red bells for 3 minutes. Add the chicken, tempeh, sea salt and chili powder. Sauté for 3 more minutes.

Coat a casserole-sized 9x13 baking pan with enchilada sauce. Take the 12 tortillas and soak in the enchilada sauce for about 10 seconds. Line the bottom of the baking pan with six tortillas. Pour the chicken mixture on top of the tortillas and evenly distribute. Add ½ of the cheese. Do a layer of the remaining soaked tortillas. Top with the last of the cheese and ½ cup of sauce. Cover with foil and bake in the oven at 350 degrees for 20 minutes. Remove foil and bake for 10 more minutes, to brown the top.

Cut baked enchiladas into squares. Garnish with cilantro and any remaining sauce.

Serves 8 -10. Enjoy!

OPTION

For a vegetarian option, substitute chicken for crumbled tempeh.

THAI BUTTERNUT SQUASH CURRY

This fresh curry is simple to prepare. It's easy to make vegetarian style or with meat. The flavor of this curry has a balance between sweet, tangy, and salty.

½ butternut squash
2 tablespoons olive oil
½ yellow onion, large diced
1 tablespoon coarsely chopped garlic
1 tablespoon peeled and coarsely chopped fresh ginger
1-14 oz can unsweetened coconut milk
4 tablespoons Thai yellow curry paste (you can use green or red curry as well)
⅔ cup water
½ cup tofu diced into ½ inch cubes
2 kaffir lime leaves*
1 stalk lemon grass, cut into 1 inch chunks*
1 tablespoon brown sugar or palm sugar
1 tablespoon fish sauce (optional)
1 teaspoon sea salt
Lemon juice to taste
¼ cup coarsely chopped cilantro leaves
¼ cup fresh whole basil leaves, picked off the stem
2 tomatoes, cut into wedges
1 bottle of Sri Racha Rooster Sauce

Trim off the stem and blossom end of the butternut squash. Halve lengthwise and scoop out and discard the seeds and fibers. Cut into large chunks and carefully peel each chunk. Cut the peeled chunks into 1-inch pieces. You will want about 2 cups of diced squash. Set aside.

In a medium saucepan, sauté the onion, garlic and ginger with oil. Shake the coconut milk can well. Pour the coconut milk into the saucepan. Cook, stirring occasionally, until the mixture thickens and releases its sweet fragrance, about 3 minutes.

Add the curry paste, and cook for 1 to 2 minutes, mashing, scraping, and stirring until the paste is dissolved into the coconut milk, and the mixture is heated through. Add the water, salt, butternut squash, tofu, kaffir leaves, lemon grass, brown sugar, fish sauce and sea salt. Raise the heat to high, and bring the curry to a rolling boil. Stir well, reduce the heat to maintain a gentle boil, and continue cooking until the squash is tender and the sauce is smooth, about 20 minutes. Taste the curry. Does it need lemon juice to balance out the sweetness of the squash? Does it need more curry? More salt? More sugar? If so, add to taste.

When the curry is cooked, add ¼ cup cilantro, ¼ cup whole basil leaves and tomato wedges. Remove from the heat and transfer to a serving bowl on top of jasmine rice. Garnish with Sri Racha sauce for additional heat and flavor. Serves 4 to 6.

OPTIONS

Substitute ½ pound boneless skinless chicken thighs for tofu, cooked and chopped. You can add other vegetables such as eggplant, red bell peppers, and potatoes.

*If you can't find kaffir lime leaves or lemon grass, you can do without. Just increase the amount of curry paste to your liking.

CHICKEN STYLE TOFU

Here is my highly coveted, super-top-secret tofu recipe. For vegetarians and vegans, this dish is the Holy Grail. If you know anything about my legacy, you will know that I require that people work for this recipe; I don't just give it out. People have to show me they want it. They have to give me something. But you are the lucky one. Turn the page to get my recipe for this fabulous dish, and use it carefully and wisely...

NO! I CAN'T DO IT!

I would hate to rob you of the fun of trading for this special recipe. This recipe has gotten me free use of a beach house, numerous foot massages and many special dances. I have received fabulous drawings like the one below. It's simply more fun for people (and me) to trade and barter for this recipe than it is to just get it for free or in exchange for money.

If you want to get the recipe, feel free to contact me at carin@culinarymagic.com and we can talk about a trade.

BAKED BEANS

2 cups dried lima beans or navy beans
¼ pound cooked and chopped bacon
1 onion, finely diced
4 tablespoons molasses
2 teaspoons sea salt
¼ teaspoon ground black pepper
2 tablespoons Dijon mustard
¼ cup ketchup or tomato paste
12 oz stout bottle of beer

Soak beans overnight in cold water. Pour out the water and cook the beans tender, approximately 45 minutes. Do not overcook. Drain and reserve the liquid.

Preheat oven to 325 degrees. Arrange the beans in a 2 quart bean pot or casserole dish by placing a portion of the beans in the bottom of dish, and layering them with chopped bacon and onion. Combine molasses, salt, pepper, mustard, ketchup, and beer. Pour over beans and stir. Pour in just enough of the reserved bean water to cover the beans. Cover the dish with a lid or aluminum foil. Bake for 1 hour.

Remove the lid and cook until the bean sauce turns a nice caramel brown, about 20 minutes. Add more liquid if necessary to prevent the beans from getting too dry. Add salt to taste. Serve with brown bread cooked in a can (pg. 128). Serves 4-6.

OPTION

To make vegetarian but get a smokey flavor, take out the bacon and add 2 teaspoons smoked paprika or chipotle instead.

FALAFEL

I learned this recipe from Nadia, a Jordanian Bedouin, who came to RDI to teach permaculture with her husband, Geoff Lawton. After I learned how to make falafel from scratch, I could never go back to the mix. It is easy to make, and it tastes so much better this way. The key is being generous with the parsley.

1 cup dry chickpeas
½ onion, diced
2 cloves of garlic, peeled
1 cup parsley leaf and stem, chopped
¼ teaspoon cayenne
1 teaspoon falafel seasoning, sumac or zatar*
1 teaspoon cumin powder
1 teaspoon sea salt
½ teaspoon baking soda

Oil for frying

Soak the chickpeas overnight in water. Drain. DO NOT COOK THE CHICKPEAS.

Combine all ingredients in a food processor. Mix thoroughly for 30 seconds.

Pour 1 inch of oil into a medium sized cast iron skillet and let heat. You can tell if the oil is hot enough by putting a slice of onion in it. If it sizzles intensely, it is ready.

With your hand, press a mound of falafel mix into a large eating spoon (I like 2-3 inch oblong spoon). Using a butter knife, gently push the mixture into the hot oil while maintaining its shape. Fry in hot oil until medium brown on one side, then flip over (about 3 minutes total). The inside can look slightly underdone. It will continue cooking as it cools.

With a slotted spoon, pull out falafel and let drain on a baking sheet covered with paper grocery bags. Serves 10-13. Serve with hummus (pg. 139), mnaish (pg. 125), and quinoa taholeh (pg. 130).

*You can get falafel seasoning, sumac or zatar in any middle-eastern market. It is not essential in this recipe, but it does make it more authentic and delicious.

PIZZA NIGHT

At nearly every course, we have a pizza party in our handmade pizza oven. The pizza oven is the hearth of RDI, where we gather to feast on homemade pizza. A Song, a Flirt, a Dance, or a Joke...These are key ingredients to a pizza party at RDI.

1

2

3

4

CHICKEN TANDOORI

1 teaspoon ground cumin powder
1 teaspoon Indian curry powder
1 teaspoon ground coriander powder
1 teaspoon paprika powder
1 teaspoon ginger powder
1 teaspoon ground cloves
1-2 teaspoon sea salt
1 cup plain yogurt
1 tablespoon lemon juice
3 tablespoons diced yellow onion
3 tablespoons olive oil
2 cloves minced garlic
3 pounds bone-in chicken thighs

Whisk all ingredients together except the chicken.

Make small cuts in the chicken (to better absorb the marinade). Pour the marinade over the chicken and let sit covered for at least 2 hours in the refrigerator (marinating overnight is ideal).

Preheat oven to 450 degrees. Put the marinated chicken in a preheated heavy pot with lid (like a Dutch oven) and cook at 450 degrees for 15 minutes (you can add all the marinade to the pot if you want to create a sauce, otherwise compost). Make sure the chicken is still pink inside. Remove lid and cook for another 5-10 minutes until the outside gets crispy and the inside is tender.

Serve with curried cauliflower with almonds (pg. 74), green salad with cardamom cashews (pg. 90) along with plain basmati rice. Serves 6-8.

< Photos on opposite page
1. Assembling the pizza.
2. Piping hot out of the oven.
3. Pizza cooks in 3-4 minutes in a hot oven.
4. Proper treatment for any chef.

PUTATOUIE *with* CREAM

This is my version of a couple of Italian classics. I add eggplant and cream to this dish because I like it that way. Technically then, this dish is not puttenesca, nor is it ratatouie. This recipe can easily be made as a meat, vegetarian, or vegan dish, by omitting or adding ingredients. I love this simple rustic dish served with creamy polenta.

1 yellow onion, diced
3 garlic cloves, minced
¼ teaspoon red pepper flakes
1 teaspoon fennel seeds
1 small eggplant, peeled and diced into ½ inch cubes
1 zucchini, sliced into ½ inch half moons
1 red bell pepper, diced into ½ inch pieces
3 tablespoons olive oil
2 tomatoes, coarsely chopped (or a 14 oz can of diced tomatoes)
2 cups red wine
⅓ cup pitted kalamata olives
2 tablespoons capers
¼ cup chopped basil
2-4 tablespoons cream
Sugar or honey to taste
Sea salt to taste
¼ cup shredded Parmesan cheese

Sauté the yellow onion, garlic, fennel seeds and red pepper flakes in olive oil until the onions are translucent. Add the eggplant and sauté for 5 minutes. Add zucchini and red bell peppers and sauté for 2 more minutes.

Add the tomatoes, red wine, olives, capers and simmer for 20 minutes with a lid on. After 20 minutes, check to see that the eggplant is cooked all the way. If so, add the basil and the cream. Add sea salt ½ teaspoon at a time. Taste. Adjust.

Sometimes with tomato-based sauces, you need to add a little sweetener to cut the acidity. Add sugar or other sweetener if it needs it. Serve on creamy polenta (pg. 129) and garnish with shredded Parmesan. Serves 6-8.

OPTION

To add meat to this dish, sauté ½ pound of ground turkey, beef, chicken thighs or Italian sausage. For extra vegetarian protein, you can add 1 cup of cooked cannellini beans instead of the meat.

TINGA TURKEY *with* FETA

I learned how to make tinga from Adriana, my friend and neighbor. She learned it from her grandmother Celia Covarrubias. When she first made it for me, I couldn't stop thinking about it, and I begged her to teach me. I have since adapted her recipe. I make tinga with turkey, chicken or beef.

3 onions, diced
4 cloves garlic, minced
2 pounds boneless turkey thighs
3 tablespoons olive oil
2 chopped tomatoes
2-4 chopped tomatillos (size should match the tomatoes)
1-2 whole chipotle peppers in adobo sauce
1 teaspoon sea salt
8 corn tortillas
¼ cup crumbled feta
8 springs cilantro

In a pot, bring 5 cups of water to a boil. Add one of the diced onions, 2 cloves of garlic and the turkey. Simmer for 30 minutes until the turkey is cooked through. Let cool. When cool, shred the turkey by hand.

In a medium pot, add the oil and bring to medium heat. Sauté the remaining onions and the garlic. Add the turkey, tomatoes, tomatillos, whole chipotles and the sea salt. Let simmer for 15 minutes until the dish becomes a stew. Add a little water the turkey was poached in if you need more juice in the pot. Warm up your tortillas. Put a scoop of tinga on soft corn tortillas. Garnish with feta and cilantro. Serves 8.

BAKED SALMON

Some of my earliest memories of eating salmon come from a place called the Salmon BBQ in Fort Bragg, California. Grilled salmon, corn on the cob, and garlic bread…it was what "summer" was. Local legend has it that 200 years ago, the salmon was so numerous in the San Francisco bay you could literally walk on them. When you live on the California coast, salmon is both a local food and a cultural legacy.

Salmon is delicious, yes, but it is also a keystone species for river ecosystems. Salmon bring rich nutrients from the ocean all way up into the mountain ecosystem. Unfortunately, our local salmon population has been struggling for a while now. For this reason, I don't eat wild salmon unless it is local. If we don't have any salmon this season, I don't eat it, as tempting as it may be to get the wild Alaskan salmon. Fortunately, the plight of the salmon is not unknown; there are many groups focused on restoring our salmon populations and waterways.

1 cup butter, melted
⅓ cup lemon juice
1 ½ teaspoon soy sauce
2 tablespoons chopped fresh parsley
1 teaspoon dry oregano
½ teaspoon garlic powder
1 teaspoon sea salt
4-6 oz salmon fillets, skin on
1 ½ teaspoon olive oil

In a bowl, mix butter, lemon juice, soy sauce, parsley, oregano, garlic powder and sea salt. Pour over salmon. Marinate salmon steaks for 1 hour. Preheat the oven to 400 degrees. Brush a baking sheet with ½ tablespoon oil. Place salmon fillets, skin side down, on prepared baking sheet. Spread marinade on top of salmon. Bake salmon until just opaque in center, about 15-20 minutes. Serves 4-6.

OPTION

This recipe works great on a barbeque grill. Brush any remaining marinade on bread and toast in the oven.

CHICKEN TAGINE

⅛ cup extra-virgin olive oil
2 medium onions, diced
2 teaspoons garlic, minced
⅓ teaspoon turmeric powder
3 medium boneless skinless chicken thighs, cut into 1 inch chunks
¼ teaspoon ginger powder
⅓ teaspoon cinnamon powder
1 cup pitted prunes or dried apricots, sliced in half
1 lemon, cut into wheels, seeds removed, rind on
Sea salt and pepper to taste
1 tablespoon toasted sesame seeds
½ bunch parsley leaves, chopped

In a thick bottomed pan over a low flame, cook onions and olive oil for 5-10 minutes, stirring occasionally until they take on a translucent appearance. Stir in the garlic, chicken, spices, prunes, salt and pepper. Place the lemons on top. Simmer tagine with a lid on the pot for about 20-30 minutes.

Garnish with toasted sesame seeds and parsley. Serve with Israeli couscous (pg. 131) as a side dish. Serves 4-6.

MOQUEKA (BRAZILIAN FISH STEW)

My Brazilian friends, Anna, Beto and Ananda, first taught me how to make a moqueka. To me, moqueka is like Thai curry without the spice. After many kitchen dance parties and test trials, I think I am starting to get the feel of it. The secret ingredient? Bossa nova or samba music while preparing it. I am serious. It absolutely makes the food taste better.

2 pounds wild cod filet, rinsed in cold water, pin bones removed, cut into 3 inch pieces
2 tablespoons olive oil
3 cloves garlic, minced
½ yellow onion, chopped fine
1-14 oz can coconut milk
1 tablespoon fish sauce (Thai fish sauce)
1 tablespoon tomato paste
Sea salt to taste
½ teaspoon red pepper flakes
4 tablespoons lime or lemon juice
1-2 teaspoon lime or lemon zest
2 tomatoes, sliced into wedges
½ red onion, sliced into half moons
1 red bell pepper, de-stemmed and chopped
¼ bunch cilantro, leaves picked
1 Brazilian album (I recommend "The Shadow of Your Smile," by Astrud Gilberto)

Preheat oven to 375 degrees. Turn on the music. Coat the fish in 1 tablespoon olive oil and put in a Pyrex baking pan. Cover and put in the fridge while preparing other ingredients.

In a pot on medium heat, add the olive oil, garlic and onions and sauté until the onions are translucent. Add the coconut milk, fish sauce, tomato paste, salt and red pepper flakes. Simmer for 15 minutes. Add the lime juice and zest. Adjust the seasonings.

Remove the fish from the fridge. Spoon the coconut sauce over the top of the fish until it is submerged in about ¼ inch in sauce. Add tomato, red bell pepper, red onions on top, and bake for 15-20 minutes until the fish is flakey but not over done. Garnish with cilantro. Serve with rice and couve (pg. 62). Serves 6.

PAELLA *with* MUSSELS, CLAMS *and* ARTICHOKE HEARTS

Some of the best mussels and clams come out of Tomales Bay, just up from RDI. You can find inexpensive paella pans in a Spanish store, selected cooking stores, or online. I like to use a vegetarian-based stock for this seafood paella because I often create a no-meat zone when I am cooking for a crowd.

PAELLA

3 tablespoons olive oil
2 tomatoes, chopped
4 cloves garlic, minced
1 red bell pepper, diced
1 cup green beans, chopped into 1 inch segments
1 cup Bomba or Calasparra rice (Arborio will do as well)
4 oz jar of artichoke hearts, drained and chopped
1 dozen mussels
1 dozen clams
¼ cup fresh or frozen peas
1 lemon, cut into wedges

BROTH

4 cups water
1 teaspoon saffron threads
Vegetarian bouillon (to taste)
Sea salt to taste

To make the broth, bring all ingredients to a simmer. The broth should be flavorful and fairly salty. Keep warm over low heat.

To make the paella: Put your 13-inch paella pan on your stove on medium heat and add oil. Sauté the tomatoes and the garlic until the tomatoes begin to dissolve, about 5 minutes. Add the red bell peppers and green beans and keep sautéing for another minute. Pour the rice in a cross formation, and stir, coating the rice. Reduce heat. Spread the rice evenly on the bottom of the pan. Gently pour in 3½ cups of your stock. DO NOT STIR THE RICE. Bring up the heat gently until you see small bubbles start in the rice water, like soft rain. Add the artichoke hearts. Allow this to continue for about 10 minutes.

Nestle the clams and mussels into the rice so that you will see them when they open. Sprinkle peas on top of the paella. Cook 5 minutes until the clams and mussels begin to open and the water has been absorbed in to the rice. Check the rice for doneness. It should be firm, yet done. Not mushy. Add remaining stock if rice is under done. When done, remove from heat and add your lemon wedges in a pretty formation. Cover with a towel or foil and let rest 5 minutes. Serves 4.

OPTION

You can add boneless chicken thighs to this recipe and sauté with the tomato.

VEGETARIAN OPTION

To make this vegetarian, remove the clams and mussels, and add 1 zucchini, chopped.

PAELLA

I have recently embarked on the study of paella, this wonderful ritual food, and I am fortunate enough to have two very excellent teachers, Michael Rauner and Paz de la Calzada. They gently point to the path of the perfect paella, and they let me know when I go astray.

From what I understand, the secrets to any good paella lie in a few key things. The first element is the rice. The rice is important. Bomba rice or Calasparra rice from Spain are both heirloom varieties of rice, and they are the rice of choice. Paella is about the texture of the rice, so once you add and coat the rice, do not stir...this is very important. You can use Arborio rice or even sushi rice if you can't get traditional paella rice. Just don't stir. Paella is not risotto; if you stir, the rice will be mushy and you will have something akin to risotto.

The second element is the saffron. In a true paella, you can taste the saffron. This is important to remember if you are tempted to add sausage, ham or olives. While flavorful, these kinds of foods can overpower the saffron, which is not good. Chicken, clams, mussels, white fish, and artichoke hearts are all great in paella, because they don't mess with the taste of the saffron. If you can't taste the saffron, you can't call it paella.

The third element is the pan. You must have the right pan. Rice in paella is steamed, not boiled, which is why you need the wide pan with low sides, and a thin curved bottom (not a skillet). Never cook anything in your paella pan other than paella, even though you might be tempted to use your pan to scramble your breakfast eggs. Also, paella is cooked on an open fire or gas where it steams, not on electric and never in an oven (where it would bake). If you finish your paella in an oven, you will give it a crispy top where it should not have one.

Fourth, paella does not include onions. There is much discussion among paella aficionados about this controversial point. Some chefs are pro onion, and some are not. But in my lineage, which comes from the son of a shipwrecked sailor who married the lighthouse keeper's daughter, onions are a no-go. The water content in the onions makes the rice too mushy for a traditional paella.

Fifth, pay attention to the stock. Make sure you have a tasty stock with plenty of salt, because the rice soaks up the salt. I use a vegetarian stock or a chicken stock. (I find fish stock a bit too fishy for me.) And be careful not to put too many lemons wedges in at the end, since the acidity of the lemons can overpower the rice. Lemons go best with a seafood paella, less with a chicken or vegetarian paella.

Lastly, there is an order to how each part of the paella is created. Each step is a deliberate act: the preparation, the fire, how the rice is poured in the pan, how the paella is mixed, how it is served, and even how the pan is cleaned. All of these are important acts. And when I focus on these steps, and do them with intention, people can feel it in the paella.

But no discussion about paella can skip over the reality of the pan. I, myself, have a giant four-foot pan that feeds an entire village. It can easily hold enough paella for 100 people. This pan is so big it has a personality of its own, and it takes as much time, care, and energy as some of my relationships.

Still, having this giant pan has forced me to cook on an open fire. And I find that it is so much better for me to cook outdoors under the open sky. It is easier to see how our food connects us to nature when we see it cooked outdoors. The trees, the sky, earth, all contribute to the flavor and energy of the food on that fire.

PAELLA

Paella continued...

Cooking paella outdoors in this giant pan has also led me to some important conclusions:

1. Paella is a community food, and it is not meant to be created alone. A proper paella requires the support of others every step of the way. I see this every time I try to load the giant pan in my car. I simply can't do it all by myself.

2. The fire you tend is at the heart of your paella. It is important that the fire be started in an intentional and focused way. This sets the tone for the entire cooking and eating experience. You can see in the photos on the previous page that we start the fire at RDI using a bow drill. It is also important to have a designated fire keeper who doesn't mind getting dirty. The fire keeper tends the fire and keeps the flame just right for each stage of the paella. This is very challenging to do on an open flame with such a big pan, but when its done right, you will get the elusive soccarot, the name for the rice when it is crispy brown on the bottom, but not burnt.

3. The pan is always an excuse for togetherness. A large paella pan can feed a large group of people, but cleaning the pan can be a community act as well. The pan takes much care to keep from rusting. It needs to be cleaned with oil and wooden spoons (you can't use water because it will rust) then needs to be coated in oil, and wrapped to protect it from moisture. Make sure you have friends willing to get on their hands and knees to help clean up afterwards.

With luck, your paella will be such a hit that people will volunteer willingly to help with clean-up.

Photos on opposite page >

1. After the fire is prepared, we are ready to begin.
2. Pouring the rice in the shape of "la cruz".
3. Coat the rice before you add the water.
4. It's ready!
5. Enjoying the fire after paella.
6. Cleaning the pan is a big part of the experience.

1

2

3

4

5

6

GRAINS

HERB BREAD ROLLS

I grew up eating these rolls, and I still find the combination of herbs and onion to be utterly delicious.

2 tablespoons active yeast
1 ½ cups warm water
6 tablespoons sugar
2 eggs
⅓ cup olive oil
2 teaspoons salt
1 teaspoon fennel seed
⅓ cup fresh parsley, chopped and packed
1 tablespoon dill weed
1 cup onion, finely chopped
Up to 7 cups white spelt flour or all-purpose flour
¼ cup melted butter

Dissolve yeast in warm water (about 90 degrees) with sugar. Stir and place in a warm spot for 5 minutes. In a mixing bowl, whisk together the oil, eggs, salt, parsley, fennel, dill weed. Check the yeast mixture. When it starts to look alive and bubbly, add the oil/egg mixture to it.

Gradually add 3 cups of the spelt flour and mix for 3 minutes, until you see elastic strands of dough begin to form in the bowl.

Add chopped onion and 3 more cups of spelt flour. Turn out the dough on a floured board and begin to knead for about 5 minutes. It will be wet dough, but if it is super sticky, add a little more flour until it is damp and wet, but not sticky.

Place the dough in a bowl with a little oil in it, cover, and let sit in a warm place until its volume has doubled, about 2 hours.

Punch down and knead for 30 seconds. Divide the dough into 14 rolls on 2 sheet pans.

Cover gently and let rise about 30 more minutes in a warm place. Butter the tops with melted butter and bake at 375 degrees for 20 minutes, or until golden brown.

OPTION

To make these rolls vegan, I recommend blending ½ cup water with 2 tablespoons flax meal in a blender. This makes a nice “eggy” goo. Substitute that for the 2 eggs, and proceed with the recipe.

THYME SESAME BREAD (MNAISH)

I like to serve this with hummus to make a meal a little more special. Mnaish is essentially pita bread with an olive oil, thyme sesame, and sumac spread on top. Sumac, a sour savory reddish spice, can be found in Middle Eastern markets.

PITA

3 cups white spelt, whole wheat spelt, or all-purpose flour
1 ½ tablespoons sugar
1 ½ teaspoon sea salt
1 ½ tablespoons active dry baking yeast
2 tablespoons olive oil
1 ½ cup warm water (not hot)

THYME-SESAME-SUMAC PASTE

½ cup dried thyme
1 tablespoon dried sumac
⅓ cup sesame seeds
⅔ cup olive oil
1 teaspoon sea salt

In a bowl, add the flour, sugar, sea salt and yeast. Mix. Add the olive oil and water and knead for 10 minutes, until the dough is smooth and elastic. It should be tacky but not sticky. Add flour or water as needed. Place dough in an oiled bowl and cover with wrap or a cloth. Allow dough to rise for 1-1 ½ hours.

Mix together the thyme sesame paste. It should be a thick paste, not loose. If it is runny, add more herbs or sumac.

Preheat oven to 450 degrees after the dough has doubled in size, punch down the dough and kneed together for about 1 minute. Divide into 12 bread rolls. Roll out with a rolling pin into small flat rounds, about ⅛ inch thick. Place on parchment paper on a baking sheet.

With a spoon, spread out about 1 teaspoon of paste on each bread, leaving a little room around the edge. Bake until the rounds begin to puff up, about 3-5 minutes. Be careful not to over cook.

BUTTER MY BISCUIT

These biscuits are so easy! The key to them is chilling the melted butter and getting the buttermilk really cold.

2 cups white spelt flour or all-purpose flour
2 teaspoons baking powder
½ teaspoon baking soda
1 teaspoon sugar
¾ teaspoon sea salt
1 cup + 2 tablespoons ice cold buttermilk*
8 tablespoons melted butter, then cooled slightly
2 tablespoons melted butter for brushing on the biscuits when cooked

Preheat the oven to 475 degrees. Lightly oil a baking sheet, or put down parchment paper. Whisk the spelt, baking powder, baking soda, sugar and sea salt in a large bowl. Combine the cold buttermilk and the 8 tablespoons cooled butter in a medium bowl, stirring until the butter forms small clumps.

Add the buttermilk mixture to the spelt mixture and stir until just mixed (do not over-mix your biscuits). Using a ¼ measuring cup, scoop out the batter and drop onto the baking sheet. Bake until the tops are golden, 12-14 minutes. Brush the tops of the biscuits with the 2 tablespoons of melted butter. Makes 10 biscuits.

OPTIONS

I like to add ¼ cup chopped scallions and ½ cup cheddar cheese to these, or 1 tablespoon fresh rosemary chopped and ½ cup shredded Parmesan cheese.

*If you do not have buttermilk on hand, you can add 1 teaspoon lemon juice to 1 cup of milk as a substitute.

WHOLE GRAIN CORNBREAD *with* MISO TAHINI SPREAD

This bread is hearty and wheat-free. I first had this at Angelica's Restaurant in New York City and have been adapting the recipe ever since.

2 ½ cups cooked brown rice
1 ½ cups rolled oats, thick
1 ½ cups cornmeal
½ tablespoon sea salt
2½ cups apple cider or apple juice
¼ cup olive oil
3 tablespoons sesame seeds

Preheat the oven to 350 degrees. In a large mixing bowl, combine the cooked rice, oats, cornmeal, sea salt, apple cider, and olive oil. Mix well. Lightly oil a 9x5 loaf pan and sprinkle with sesame seeds. The seeds keep the bread from sticking to the pan.

Fill the pan with batter, smoothing the top with a spatula.

Bake in the middle rack of the oven for 1 hour and 15 minutes or until a toothpick comes out clean. Allow to cool in the pan. Serve with tahini miso spread and garnish with shredded carrots, sprouts, scallions or beets. Eat with soup! Serves 8-10.

TAHINI MISO SPREAD

3 tablespoons mellow barley miso or a chickpea miso
2 tablespoons water
⅔ cup tahini

Mix the miso and water in a blender and blend until smooth. Add tahini and process until smooth.

BROWN BREAD COOKED *in a* CAN

This method of steaming the bread on a fire is a great way to make bread when camping or on the road. I grew up eating this with baked beans. (You can also bake this bread like regular quick bread in the oven.)

1 cup yellow cornmeal
1 cup white spelt flour or all-purpose flour
1 cup rye flour
1 teaspoon baking soda
1 teaspoon sea salt
¾ cup molasses
1 ½ cup buttermilk
1 tablespoon melted butter

Steam: Melt one tablespoon butter and spread over the inside of the cans. Mix dry ingredients into the wet ingredients, and pour the mixture into three clean 14 oz cans. Cover each can with foil, and tie the foil with twine to form a tight lid. Put the cans in a water bath where the water goes ½ way up the can and boil this on the stovetop for 40 minutes. Check for doneness by sticking a knife in the bread and see if any dough comes off on the knife. When done, let cool and remove from can. Slather with butter.

OR

Bake: Melt one tablespoon butter and pour into a medium-sized cast iron skillet. Mix wet and dry ingredients as directed above and pour the mixture into the skillet. Bake at 350 degrees for about 30-40 minutes. Check for doneness by sticking a knife or toothpick in the bread and see if any dough comes off on the knife.

Serve hot with baked beans (pg. 105). Serves 8-10.

OPTION

To make vegan and gluten free, use 1 ½ cup cornmeal , 1 ½ cup Bob's Gluten Free mix, and ½ teaspoon xanthan gum (omit the rye flour). Use 1 cup almond milk (or other milk substitute) plus 1 tablespoon white vinegar (omit the buttermilk), and 2 tablespoons oil. Steam or bake.

POLENTA

Quite simply, polenta is cracked corn. It is a staple dish of Northern Italy that can be dressed up in a myriad of ways—topped with meat, fish, pasta sauce, cheese, or vegetables. I like polenta for breakfast (with a little maple syrup & fruit), lunch or dinner. Here is the most basic way to prepare polenta.

½ cup polenta
2 ½ cups water
1 teaspoon sea salt

In a pot, bring the water to a boil. Slowly whisk in the polenta and salt and keep stirring. Reduce to a simmer and stir the polenta every minute or so for 20 minutes. Remove from heat and serve with putatouie (pg. 110). Serves 2.

VARIATION 1

You can take this cooked polenta and pour it out on a greased baking sheet. When this cools, you can cut it into squares and eat like that, or reheat with cheese on top.

VARIATION 2

Substitute 1 cup of milk for water in the polenta to make it creamy and delicious.

◇◇

POLENTA PIZZA

You can add any toppings you like on this pizza, but here is a simple pizza below. This is great for folks who don't want to eat wheat, but love their pizza.

1 baking sheet cooled polenta
1 cup marinara sauce
1 cup shredded mozzarella
¼ cup shredded Parmesan
1 red bell pepper, sliced into strips
¼ cup olives, pitted and cut in half

Evenly spread marinara on the polenta. Top with cheese, red bells, and olives. Bake at 350 for 20 minutes until cheese is melted and the polenta is hot.

QUINOA TABOLEH

Though traditionally taboleh is made with bulgar wheat, I like to make taboleh with quinoa to create a wheat-free whole grain option. Quinoa taboleh served with hummus is a delicious combination.

1 cup quinoa
2 ¼ cups water
Pinch of sea salt
½ cup minced parsley
2 tablespoons minced fresh mint or 1 teaspoon dried mint
1 medium sized tomato, diced
½ cucumber, sliced into quarter moons
1 tablespoon lemon juice
¼ cup extra-virgin olive oil
¼ bunch scallion, chopped finely
½ teaspoon sea salt

Cook quinoa in 2¼ cups water and a pinch of salt for 20 minutes. Turn off heat and let cool. Finely chop the parsley and mint. Mix in quinoa, lemon juice, olive oil, parsley, mint, tomato, cucumber, scallion and sea salt. Serves 4-6.

ORZO SALAD *with* KALAMATA OLIVES, FETA, BASIL, *and* PINENUTS

One winter, I met a woman who was helping to preserve the Pinyon pinenut trees in Nevada. She informed me that due to weather changes, the Pinyon pinenut trees are having difficulty surviving, and that there are groups of volunteers helping to seed Pinyon pine trees in colder climates. Now, whenever I eat pinenuts, I think about this group of dedicated people trying to help the trees.

½ pound orzo pasta
¼ cup kalamata olives, pitted and sliced
3 tablespoons feta, crumbled
½ bunch fresh basil, sliced finely
3 tablespoons pine nuts, toasted lightly
3 tablespoons sun dried tomatoes in oil, sliced finely
2 tablespoons olive oil
2-4 tablespoons balsamic vinegar (to taste)
1-2 teaspoons sea salt (to taste)

Bring a pot of water to a boil. Boil orzo for 7-10 minutes, or until al dente. Strain pasta and rinse with cool water. Toss pasta with olives, feta, basil, pine nuts, tomatoes, olive oil, balsamic vinegar and salt. Serves 6.

ISRAELI COUSCOUS *with* FETA, PINENUTS, RAISINS, *and* SAGE

Israeli couscous is different than regular couscous. Israeli couscous is traditionally hand rolled, and it looks like little balls when cooked. I find its taste and texture very appealing.

1 cup Israeli couscous
3 cups water
Pinch of sea salt
1 tablespoon olive oil
1 yellow onion, diced
2 cloves garlic, minced
1 teaspoon dried sage
Juice of one lemon
½ cup feta cheese, crumbled
2 tablespoons pinenuts, toasted
2 tablespoons raisins
Sea salt and pepper to taste
1 tablespoon parsley leaves

Boil the water and pour couscous in it with a pinch of sea salt. Cook until couscous is al dente (3-5 minutes). Drain couscous and rinse with cold water. Set aside.

Heat up the olive oil and sauté the onions and sugar in a small pan. When they are nice and brown, add the garlic and sage and sauté for 2 minutes. Add the cooked couscous and sauté for 2 minutes. Add the feta, pinenuts and raisins, lemon juice, sea salt, and pepper. Toss. Garnish with parsley. Serve warm or cold. Serves 4-6.

BUCATINI *with* **GOAT MILK, SMOKED CHICKEN,** *and* **SPINACH**

Every day on the farm we get fresh goat's milk. This goat's milk sauce served with Bucatini pasta is a great combination. Bucatini is like spaghetti with a tube down the middle that allows the pasta to soak up all the sauce.

4 tablespoons salted butter
1 ½ sliced onions
1 teaspoon red chili flakes
½ pound smoked chicken, cut in strips
¼ pound pre-washed spinach
Zest from 2 lemons
2 cups goat milk
2 cups shredded Parmesan cheese
Sea Salt and pepper to taste
1 pound bucatini pasta
10 cherry tomatoes, sliced in half

Bring a large pot of salted water to boil. Sauté onion in butter until translucent. Add red chili flakes, chicken and cook for 1 minute. Add lemon zest, goat milk, and Parmesan. Bring to a gentle simmer and cook, stirring occasionally until slightly thickened, about 5-10 minutes. Season with salt and pepper. Meanwhile, cook pasta until al dente. Drain pasta, add to mixture, and stir to combine and heat through. Serve immediately with halved cherry tomatoes. Serves 6.

OPTION

You can substitute cream for goat's milk in this recipe. To make gluten free, you can easily substitute bucatini for gluten free pasta.

DIPS AND APPETIZERS

FIRE ROASTED SALSA

On the farm there are some extremely hot manzano chili peppers that grow in the green house that I like to use in this salsa. When you make this, adjust the spice level to your liking.

1 tablespoon olive oil
2 red bells, deseeded and cut in half
1 red onion, peeled and cut in half
2 medium tomatoes, whole
10 cloves of garlic, peeled
½ garden manzano chili, or jalapeno, deseeded
¼ teaspoon cayenne pepper
¼ teaspoon chipotle powder
2-4 tablespoons lime juice
1 teaspoon sea salt

Heat the oil in a cast iron pan over a medium heat. Add the red bell peppers, onion, tomatoes, garlic and manzano and let cook until blackened. You will have to pull out the garlic and manzano first (they blacken the fastest). Place the blackened ingredients in a food processor. Add cayenne, chipotle powder, 2 tablespoons lime juice and the salt. Blend. Taste and adjust sea salt, lime, or chipotle. Makes 3 cups.

◇◇

TETE'S MOHAMMARA

This is one of the most unusual and delicious dips. I learned this from my mother's mother-in-law, Tete, and her dip is how I fell in love with pomegranate molasses.

2 cups walnuts
1 red onion, chopped
2 red bells, de-seeded and chopped
2 tablespoons tahini
2 tablespoons paprika
3 tablespoons lemon juice
2 tablespoons pomegranate molasses
¼ cup water
1 teaspoon cumin powder
1½ teaspoon sea salt
Extra-virgin olive oil

In a 350 degree oven, roast the walnuts for 6-8 minutes until they are a shade darker. Let cool for five minutes. In a food processor add the red onion, red bell peppers, lemon juice, walnuts, tahini, and paprika. Mix. Add lemon juice, pomegranate molasses, water, cumin and sea salt. Grind together, then adjust the seasonings. Pour onto a plate. Top with extra-virgin olive oil and drizzle with pomegranate molasses. Serve with mnaish (pg. 125). Makes 6 cups.

COCONUT CHUTNEY

1 cup unsweetened shredded coconut
1 tablespoon minced ginger
3 tablespoons onion, chopped
½ small green chili (optional)
½ teaspoon sea salt
1 teaspoon brown sugar
1½ tablespoon lemon juice
⅛ - ¼ cup hot water
1½ teaspoons olive oil
1 teaspoon brown mustard seeds

In a blender, combine all the ingredients except the olive oil and mustard seeds. Use enough hot water to easily blend the chutney ingredients into a thick smooth paste.

Heat the oil in a small, heavy pan and add the mustard seeds. They will pop frantically. The moment the popping dies down, add the chutney. Rinse the blender, using about ¼ cup hot water, and add to the chutney. Reduce the heat and bring the chutney to a simmer for 5 minutes.

Use the chutney right away or store in a glass jar in the refrigerator. The chutney will last for several weeks in the refrigerator. Makes 2 cups. Serve with tandoori chicken (pg. 109), curried cauliflower (pg. 74), coconut mung dahl (pg. 50) and basmati rice.

◇◇

AJI AMARILLO SAUCE

I first tasted this bright garlic sauce on quinoa on a mountaintop high in the Andes. It's excellent on top of quinoa (pg. 130) served with Peruvian roast chicken (pg.96) and the Peruvian salad (pg. 86). You can get aji amarillo chilies in Latin markets and some health food stores.

2 tablespoons minced onion
1 tablespoon lime juice or white vinegar
2 tablespoons Parmesan cheese, grated
2 tablespoons fresh minced cilantro
½ jalapeno pepper, deseeded and chopped
2 garlic cloves, minced
3 aji amarillo chilies, soaked and chopped*
1 teaspoon sea salt
1 cup organic mayonnaise

Put all the ingredients in a blender, and mix until smooth and creamy. Adjust salt and lime to taste. Makes 1½ cup sauce.

*If you can't find aji amarillo chilies, you can add 1 teaspoon turmeric powder instead.

HUMMUS

The first contact I ever had with hummus was at a Grateful Dead concert in Long Beach, CA. There was a beautiful shirtless man wearing a colorful Indian skirt. He had a box on his head with a red balloon tied to it. On the box it said, "Hummus Sandwich, $2.00. The man was spinning around and around with a big smile on his face. I asked my friend, "What exactly is hummus?" I have never been the same since.

Hummus has now entered the mainstream. You can go to almost any party and find hummus on the table. But not all hummus is the same. Some is traditional. Some is modern. Some is made with garbanzo beans. Some is made with edamame. My mom taught me that even a simple dish like hummus could be turned into a work of art. In addition, she married someone from Syria, so this recipe comes from her mother-in law, Tete. Here is the recipe she gave me:

1 cup dry garbanzo beans (about 3 cups cooked beans)
¼ teaspoon baking soda
3 cloves garlic
⅓ cup fresh lemon juice
½ cup tahini
1 ½ teaspoon sea salt

Soak 1 cup of garbanzo beans overnight. Drain. Transfer to a medium sized pot. Cover with filtered water, plus 2 inches extra. Bring to a boil. Add ½ teaspoon baking soda to alkalinize and tenderize the beans. This also "sweetens" the beans slightly.

Boil one hour with lid on. If any thick foam appears, scoop it off the top. Uncover. Continue to cook rapidly, adding water until the beans are soft and well done. Important: There must be bean-water left over. Do not throw this bean-water out. Do not salt during cooking. Save 3/4 cup liquid from the beans. Let beans and bean-water cool.

In a blender add garlic, lemon juice, and tahini. Blend for about 20 seconds. Add 2 cups cooked beans, 3/4 cup bean water, and sea salt. Grind in blender for a few minutes, until mixed through and creamy. Use a wooden spoon to help the hummus mix well while blending. Add beans or liquid as needed.

Immediately pour into a concave or flat dish with a little side on it. Hummus should be fairly fluid and "ripple" just after it has been poured. This is the sign of authenticity. Save out a large spoonful of un-ground cooked beans and use them as garnish them in the middle of the plate.

Good decorations include olives, strips of pepper, designs with black pepper, cumin, sumac, allspice, paprika OR only just clumps of pomegranate seeds or pomegranate molasses. Top with a drizzle of extra-virgin olive oil. Serve with mnaish (pg. 125) or pita bread. Makes 3 cups.

LENTIL WALNUT PATE

This unusual vegetarian dip is satisfying and delicious. You can find umeboshi at most health food stores, and can substitute barley miso for sweet miso.

⅔ cup dried red or green lentils, rinsed
2 cups walnuts
1 tablespoon extra-virgin olive oil
3 cups diced onions
1 tablespoon minced garlic
1 tablespoon mirin
1 tablespoon plus 1 teaspoon umeboshi paste
1 ½ tablespoon barley miso
1 tablespoon dried basil

Preheat oven to 350 degrees. Rinse lentils in strainer under cold running water. Place lentils in a 2-quart saucepan with enough water to cover them by 2 inches. Bring to a boil. Lower heat, cover and simmer until the lentils are tender, about 30 to 40 minutes. When lentils are tender, remove from heat and drain.

Roast the walnuts on a cookie sheet at 350 until they turn a shade darker, about 6 to 8 minutes. Pour the nuts into a colander and let them cool. Sauté the onions and garlic in olive oil in an 8 inch skillet over a medium flame, stirring frequently, until lightly browned, about 10 to 15 minutes.

Combine the lentils, walnuts, onion mixture, and remaining ingredients in a food processor fitted with a steel blade and puree until smooth. Spoon into a bowl and refrigerate until cool. The pate will keep 3 to 5 days refrigerated in a tightly sealed container. Makes 6 cups.

BUFFY APPLE BUTTER

I like to make apple butter every year with my neighbor and permaculture visionary, Starhawk. We have a standing date to watch Buffy the Vampire Slayer while the apples are cooking for hours and hours.

20 apples, cored and quartered (you don't need to peel them if they are organic)
1 cup apple cider
4 tablespoons Calvados, French apple brandy (optional, also, regular brandy can be substituted)
4 cinnamon sticks
1 tablespoon ground ginger
1 teaspoon cardamom powder
1 teaspoon ground nutmeg
1 teaspoon ground cloves
1 cup sugar
2 tablespoons lemon juice
1 Buffy CD

Combine apples, cider, calvados, cinnamon, ginger, cardamom, nutmeg, cloves, sugar and lemon juice in a large heavy-bottomed pot. Place over medium high heat and cook, stirring occasionally with a large spoon to prevent from sticking. Put on an episode of Buffy. When the apples are mushy, put Buffy on pause.

Heat the oven to 300 degrees. Remove the cinnamon sticks, and blend up the apple mush in a food processor until smooth and creamy. Put the apple mush in a baking pan and place in the oven for another 3+ hours until the butter is reduced and a nice brown. Finish watching your show. You can store your apple butter in the fridge for up to one month, or in the freezer for 6 months.

IT'S OK IF WE MESS UP

It's OK if we mess up. Really, I mean it. Burning, over cooking, under cooking, putting in too much (or too little), and dropping things are all part of the process of learning how to cook and focusing our awareness. It can be upsetting when mishaps occur, but they happen to everyone. And what an opportunity to be kind to ourselves! What a chance to refocus!

Those little accidents call us to be in the present moment. Little by little, we learn about food, and we learn about ourselves. We begin where we are, and we learn how to trust ourselves to make something well. And even if we do something we are not supposed to do, it usually works out fine.

I once taught a class with students who had a complete fear of cooking and zero experience. They were in charge of making an entire lasagna meal, and each and every one of them felt lost and overwhelmed. I gave them only concepts and ingredients—sauce, pasta, cheese, veggies, sauce, pasta, cheese—no exact recipe. I had experienced cooks in the class to help, but they were not allowed to give any advice. Their only job was to support the new cooks' thinking and intuition.

We all bit our tongues as we watched these new cooks put whole basil stems into the marinara sauce, or large chunks of onion instead of the minced version. We all waited in anticipation as that lasagna cooked, wondering how it would turn out. Would it hold together? Would it look decent? Would it even be edible? As it turned out, it wasn't the best lasagna ever made, but it was far from the worst. It was perfectly edible, and we all truly enjoyed it. And as a result, those cooks who had once been so afraid, now make their own food with peaceful regularity.

We all have to start where we are—experienced, inexperienced, having a good day, having a bad one. And when the inevitable mistake happens, I ask that you take it in stride, and don't apologize about it to your diners. For them, your "accident" could be precisely the kind of meal they want and need. It could taste wonderful to them. You don't want to diminish their experience by bemoaning the fact that you didn't do something perfectly. Breathe. And with a straight and proud face, tell your friends what you made, and let them enjoy it. Be good to yourself. And keep cooking.

Oops, I burnt the granola! >

DESSERTS

CHOCOLATE CHERRY OATMEAL COOKIES

ROSE HIP PIE

APPLE PIE

PEACH COBBLER WITH LEMON CORNMEAL TOPPING

CARROT CAKE WITH MAPLE FROSTING

STRAWBERRY SHORTCAKE

STRAWBERRY BUTTERMILK CAKE

CARDAMOM BANANA CAKE
WITH COCONUT CREAM FROSTING

PUMPKIN CAKE WITH CHOCOLATE-ALMOND GANACHE

JAM DOTS

VEGAN CHOCOLATE CAKE WITH RASPBERRY COULIS

THE GOO!

CHOCOLATE CHERRY OATMEAL COOKIES *with* PECANS

1 ¼ cup spelt flour or all-purpose flour
¾ teaspoon baking powder
½ teaspoon baking soda
½ teaspoon sea salt
1 ¼ cups rolled oats
1 cup pecans (or walnuts) toasted and chopped*
1 cup dried cherries, rough chopped*
¾ cup chocolate chips
1 ½ stick unsalted butter, softened
1 ½ cups brown sugar
1 large egg
1 teaspoon vanilla extract

Heat oven to 350 degrees. Grease 2 cookie sheets. Whisk flour, baking powder, baking soda, and salt in a bowl. Add oats, pecans, cherries and chocolate chips.

In a separate bowl with an electric mixer, beat the butter and sugar until no lumps remain (about 1 minute). Add egg and vanilla and mix. Gradually add the flour mixture until mixed. Divide dough into 20 cookies, and roll into balls. Place on baking sheets and press balls to one-inch thickness. Bake for 12 minutes, pull out cookies and rotate, and cook for 5 minutes longer, or until the cookies are medium brown but the centers seem wet. Let cool.

*If you choose not to add nuts to this recipe, add 1 extra cup of oats to the batter to hold the cookies together. The nuts add structure to the cookie so you need something to keep the batter together.

*If you don't have dried cherries on hand, you can substitute raisins, dried apricots, or any other dried fruit.

OPTION

To make this gluten free, you can use Bob's Gluten Free Flour mix and ½ teaspoon xanathan gum.

VEGAN OPTION

Substitute the butter for non-hydrogenated shortening, and ½ flax seed mixture (pg. 159) for eggs.

ROSE HIP PIE *with* ROSE CREAM

I love this unusual old-fashioned use of rose hips. A rose hip is the fruit of the rose. Rose hips have tons of vitamin C and are amazingly delicious. Get the seedless kind. They get super squishy after they have been soaked for an hour. I like to use a pecan or walnut crust with this recipe, or a classic pastry crust works great too.

ROSE HIP FILLING

1 cup dried seedless rosehips, soaked for 1 hour in 1 ½ cups of water and then pureed
¾ cup sugar
½ teaspoon vanilla extract
1 teaspoon cinnamon
1 tablespoon minced fresh ginger, or 1 teaspoon ginger powder
¼ teaspoon ground nutmeg
1 teaspoon ground allspice
2 eggs
½ cup soy, almond, goat or cow milk

Preheat the oven to 350 degrees. In a food processor or blender, combine 1 ½ cup rose hip puree, sugar, vanilla, cinnamon, ginger, nutmeg, allspice, milk and eggs, in batches if necessary. Process until the mixture is well combined and smooth. Mix the pie crust ingredients together, and press the pie crust mixture into the bottom of a greased pie pan. Pour the liquid rose hip mixture into the pie crust and bake for 50 minutes, or until the filling has firmed up. Sometimes you will see the filling start to form cracks in it, which tells you it is getting firmer. Let cool. Serve with rose cream. Serves 6.

PECAN OR WALNUT CRUST

1 cup oats, ground
1 cup pecans or walnuts, ground
1 cup spelt flour or all-purpose flour
½ cup maple syrup
⅓ cup rice or sunflower oil
¼ teaspoon sea salt

APPLE PIE *with* OAT ALMOND CRUST

When I was in college, I used to make apple pies. I would dumpster-dive the dry good ingredients, and get the apples at the farmers market at the end of the day. I would then sell the pies at Grateful Dead shows in the parking lot at the Oakland Coliseum for $2 a slice. This apple pie has a wholesome feel to it. Plus, it's easy to make.

APPLE FILLING

2 pounds apples, 6 apples, or about 7 cups, core removed and sliced (each half cut into eighths)
4 tablespoons arrowroot powder or cornstarch
1 teaspoon cinnamon
½ teaspoon nutmeg
¼ teaspoon sea salt
¾ cup sugar
3 tablespoons lemon juice

Mix all the ingredients together and set aside.

OAT ALMOND CRUST

1 cup oats, ground
1 cup almonds, ground
1 cup spelt flour or all purpose flour
⅓ cup maple syrup
⅓ cup rice or sunflower oil
¼ teaspoon sea salt

Mix all the ingredients together and set aside.

Preheat the oven to 350 degrees. Grease the pie pan. Press ⅔ of the crust mixture into the pie pan, fill with apple filling, then sprinkle the rest of the crust on the top. Cook for about 40 minutes until bubbly. Serves 6.

OPTION

To make this recipe gluten free, you can substitute rice flour for spelt. You can also substitute sunflower seeds or walnuts for almonds.

PEACH COBBLER *with* LEMON CORNMEAL TOPPING

FILLING

2 ½ pounds ripe peaches (6-7)
¼ cup sugar
1 teaspoon cornstarch or arrowroot
1 tablespoon fresh lemon juice
Pinch of sea salt

BISCUIT TOPPING

1 cup minus 2 tablespoons white spelt flour or unbleached pastry flour
2 tablespoons cornmeal
1 tablespoon lemon zest
3 tablespoons sugar
¾ teaspoon baking powder
¼ teaspoon baking soda
¼ teaspoon sea salt
5 tablespoons cold unsalted butter, cut into ¼ inch cubes
⅓ cup whole yogurt

FOR THE FILLING

Preheat oven to 425 degrees.

Halve and pit each peach. Cut each half into 4 wedges. Gently toss peaches and sugar together in a large bowl. Let stand for 30 minutes. Drain peaches, retaining the juice.

Mix ¼ cup of the peach juice with the cornstarch, lemon juice and salt. Toss this juice mixture in with the peaches and transfer to a 10-inch square baking pan. Place in oven and cook for 10 minutes.

FOR THE TOPPING

In a food processor, gently pulse flour, sugar, baking soda, baking powder, and salt. Add butter and pulse until the batter looks crumbly. Transfer to a bowl, add yogurt and toss until a dough forms. Separate the dough into 6 equal shaped mounds. Place the dough mounds on top of the pre-cooked peaches, spacing them evenly.

Sprinkle each dough mound with a little sugar. Bake until the topping is brown, and the peaches are bubbling, about 20-25 minutes. Let cool until warm, then serve. Serves 6.

CARROT CAKE *with* MAPLE WHIPPED CREAM CHEESE FROSTING

2 cups spelt flour or all-purpose flour*
2 teaspoons baking soda
1 teaspoon sea salt
1 teaspoon ground cinnamon
2 cups sugar
1 ¼ cups canola oil
4 large eggs
3 cups grated carrots
1 ¼ cups coarsely chopped walnuts
1 tablespoon ginger powder
12 toasted walnut halves (for garnish)

Preheat oven to 350 degrees. Butter two 9-inch-diameter cake pans. Butter and flour the pans, tap out flour.

Whisk flour, baking soda, salt and cinnamon in medium bowl to blend. Whisk sugar and oil in large bowl until well blended. Whisk in eggs 1 at a time. Add flour mixture and stir until blended. Stir in carrots, walnuts and ginger. Divide batter between prepared pans.

Bake cakes until tester inserted into center comes out clean, about 40 minutes. Cool cakes in pans 15 minutes. Turn out onto racks. Cool cakes completely.

Place 1 cake layer on a platter. Spread with 3/4 cup maple whipped cream cheese frosting. Top with second layer. Spread remaining frosting over entire cake. Arrange walnut halves around top edge.

*Gluten Free Variation: You can substitute Bob's Gluten Free Flour Mix and ½ teaspoon xanthan gum for spelt or all-purpose flour in this recipe.

MAPLE WHIPPED CREAM CHEESE FROSTING

10 ounces cream cheese, room temperature
1 cup heavy cream, cold
2 tablespoons brown sugar
2 tablespoons pure maple syrup

Using an electric mixer or a food processor, beat cream cheese with ¼ cup heavy cream until smooth with no lumps. Remove from mixing bowl. In a clean bowl, add remaining heavy cream with sugar and maple syrup and beat until fluffy whipped cream.

Gently fold the whipped cream into the creamed cream cheese. Do not over mix.

STRAWBERRY SHORTCAKE *with* ALMOND PRALINES *and* ROSE CREAM

This recipe has 5 simple parts: the biscuit, strawberry sauce, strawberry topping, rose whipped cream, and almond pralines. Put them together to make a delicious dessert.

THE BISCUIT

2 cups white spelt or all-purpose flour
2 teaspoons baking powder
½ teaspoon baking soda
1 tablespoon sugar
¾ teaspoon sea salt
1 cup + 2 tablespoons cold buttermilk
8 tablespoons butter, melted, then cooled slightly
2 tablespoons melted butter for brushing on the biscuits when cooked

Preheat the oven to 475 degrees. On a baking sheet, put down parchment paper or lightly oil. Whisk the spelt (flour), baking powder, baking soda, sugar and sea salt in a large bowl. Combine the cold buttermilk and the 8 tablespoons cooled butter in a medium bowl, stirring until the butter forms small clumps.

Add the buttermilk mixture to the spelt mixture and stir until just mixed (do not over mix your biscuits). Using a ¼ measuring cup, scoop out the batter and drop onto the baking sheet. Bake 12-14 minutes or until the tops are golden. Brush the tops of the biscuits with the 2 tablespoons of melted butter.

STRAWBERRY SAUCE

1 pint strawberries, de-stemmed
2-3 tablespoons maple syrup, brown sugar, or agave
1 ½ teaspoons lemon juice
1 ¼ teaspoon vanilla extract
Pinch sea salt

Puree all ingredients in the blender.

STRAWBERRY TOPPING

1 pint strawberries
1-3 tablespoons maple sugar, brown sugar, or white sugar
Fresh mint for garnish

Slice strawberries in half, add the sugar and let sit for at least 1 hour.

Strawberry Shortcake recipe continues on the following page...

Strawberry Shortcake continued...

ROSE WHIPPED CREAM

1 cup whipping cream
2 tablespoons maple syrup or brown sugar
½ teaspoon rose water

Beat all ingredients in a hand mixer until firm waves form in the cream.

ALMOND PRALINES

1 cup almonds, slivered
2 tablespoons maple syrup
2 tablespoons maple sugar or brown sugar

Preheat oven to 350. In a small bowl, combine nuts, maple syrup and maple sugar. Mix well. Spread maple nut mixture on a cookie sheet and bake for 15 minutes, stirring occasionally. Scrape pralines onto a plate and cool until crunchy.

TO ASSEMBLE

Pour 2 tablespoons of strawberry sauce on to each plate. Slice biscuit in half horizontally and place bottom half on top of the sauce. Put a spoon of strawberry topping on the biscuit. Top with the biscuit top. Pour more strawberry sauce on top. Add a dollop of rose whipped cream and another spoonful of strawberry topping. Garnish with a mint leaf and almond pralines.

STRAWBERRY BUTTERMILK CAKE

The texture of this simple cake is so delicious. The secret to the texture is following the directions on how to mix the batter.

BUTTERMILK CAKE

2 ⅓ cups white spelt or unbleached flour, sifted
1 ½ teaspoon baking powder
½ teaspoon baking soda
¼ teaspoon sea salt
¾ cup softened unsalted butter
1 ⅓ cups sugar
3 eggs
1 teaspoon vanilla
1 cup buttermilk
15 strawberries, sliced

Preheat oven to 350. Grease up two 9-inch cake pans. Whisk together the dry ingredients. In a mixing bowl, beat the butter. Gradually add the sugar and beat for about 3-5 minutes.

Slowly beat in 3 large eggs and vanilla.

At low speed, add the flour slowly, alternating with the buttermilk. Beat until smooth. Divide the batter between the pans and top with sliced strawberries. Bake 35-40 minutes. Test for doneness by inserting a toothpick into the cake. If it comes out clean, it is done. Let cool and remove from pan. Frost the layers with maple whipped cream cheese frosting (pg. 151). Serves 8.

CARDAMOM BANANA CAKE *with* COCONUT CREAM FROSTING

2 cups white spelt or all-purpose flour
1 teaspoon baking soda
1 teaspoon baking powder
1 teaspoon sea salt
2 teaspoons ground cardamom
½ cup rice oil or sunflower oil
½ cup buttermilk*
1 ¼ cups mashed super ripe bananas
2 eggs
1 ½ cup sugar
½ cup chopped and toasted walnuts

COCONUT CREAM FROSTING

6 egg yolks
10 tablespoons sugar
6 tablespoons spelt or all-purpose flour
2 cups milk, heated
4 tablespoons unsalted butter
2 teaspoons vanilla extract
¼ teaspoon sea salt
1 cup unsweetened shredded coconut

Sift together flour, baking soda, baking powder, salt, and cardamom. Place in a large bowl. Add oil, buttermilk and bananas. Whisk or blend for about 30 seconds. In a separate bowl, beat 2 eggs until foamy. Add sugar and continue beating for 3 minutes. Add walnuts.

Fold egg-sugar mixture into batter. Pour into 2-9inch round pans. Lightly bang the full pans on the counter, to remove the bubbles. Bake at 350 degrees for 30 minutes. Let cool. Run a knife along the edge of the pan to loosen the cake, and turn out.

For the cream beat the yolks and sugar together. Add the flour and continue to beat until blended. Add heated milk and place pan over heat, stirring until the mixture is thickened. The mixture can come to a brief boil. Keep stirring. Remove from the heat and stir in the butter, vanilla, sea salt, and coconut.

You can layer the cakes and frost the middle and the top of this cake.

*If you don't have buttermilk on hand, you can add 1 teaspoon lemon juice to ½ cup milk as a substitute.

OPTION

For gluten free substitute 2 cups of Bob's Gluten Free Flour for spelt flour, and add ½ teaspoon xanthan gum. Substitute 3 tablespoons corn or arrowroot starch for wheat flour in the frosting recipe.

PUMPKIN CAKE *with* CHOCOLATE-ALMOND GANACHE

PUMPKIN CAKE

1 ¾ cups spelt or all-purpose flour
1 teaspoon baking soda
¾ teaspoon sea salt
¼ teaspoon nutmeg
½ teaspoon cloves
1 teaspoon cinnamon
1 teaspoon ginger
1 ½ cups sugar
½ cup vegetable oil
⅓ cup water
2 eggs
1 cup pumpkin puree*

Sift dry ingredients together in a large bowl and set aside. Mix pumpkin water, oil and eggs together. Pour into dry ingredients and mix well. Pour into 2 greased loaf pans. Bake at 350 degrees for one hour. Cool 15 minutes before removing from pans.

*You can use pumpkin puree from a can, or make your own by baking a pumpkin or yam, scooping out the insides, and pureeing it in a blender with a little water.

GLUTEN FREE OPTION

To make this gluten free, substitute Bob's Gluten Free Flour and 1 teaspoon xanthan gum for the spelt flour.

VEGAN OPTION

To make this vegan, substitute 2 tablespoons flax meal blended with ½ cup water for the eggs.

CHOCOLATE-ALMOND GANACHE

1 cup almonds
2 cups almond milk
1 pound semisweet chocolate chips, melted

In a blender, grind the almonds with the almond milk. Add the melted chocolate and blend until smooth. Pour in a bowl and let refrigerate for 4-6 hours. When it has set, frost your cake.

VEGAN BAKING

It is easy to substitute non-hydrogenated shortening for butter, and flax seed for eggs in many of the recipes. Here is a way to make a great egg substitute for most of your baked bread items:

¼ cup whole flax seeds
1 cup warm water

In a blender, add these ingredients and blend for 45 seconds. You will notice the mixture will become egg-like in texture. Use ¼ cup of this mixture to substitute for 1 egg.

◇◇

JAM DOTS

This was one of the first healthy desserts I ever learned how to make. These are delicious to eat, easy to make, have few ingredients, are naturally vegan, and everybody loves them.

1 cup rolled oats
1 cup almonds
1 cup white spelt flour
½ cup maple syrup
⅓ cup light vegetable oil (rice oil, sunflower oil)
¼ teaspoon sea salt
Your favorite fruit jam

Preheat oven to 350 degrees. In the food processor, blend the oats to make coarse flour. Pour into a bowl. Next, blend the almonds to a course meal and pour into the same bowl. Add the spelt flour. Add the maple syrup, oil and sea salt. Mix together. Roll the dough into 12-14 balls and put on cookie sheet. With your thumb, make small little "wells" in the dough. With a teaspoon, fill the wells with jam. Bake for 12-15 minutes until the jam begins to bubble.

OPTION

To make gluten free jam dots, substitute rice flour for the spelt flour.

VEGAN CHOCOLATE CAKE *with* RASPBERRY COULIS *and* VEGAN CHOCOLATE ICING

So what is a coulis (pronounced "cool lee"), you might ask? Basically, it's a blended fruit sauce. The redness of the raspberry with the dark chocolate color is quite pleasing visually, and the combination tastes delicious. The vegan chocolate cake recipe below is one that I use as a base for many different chocolate cakes.

THE CAKE

3 cups white spelt or all-purpose flour
⅔ cups unsweetened cocoa powder, sifted (must sift!)
2 teaspoons baking soda
2 cups sugar
1 teaspoon sea salt
2 cups cold water
½ cup + 2 tablespoons rice or sunflower oil
1 tablespoon vanilla
2 tablespoons white vinegar or lemon juice

Mix together flour, cocoa, baking soda, sugar, and salt. Sift. In separate bowl, mix together water, oil, vanilla, and vinegar or lemon.

Whisk together the wet and dry ingredients. Pour through strainer into a bowl, breaking up lumps and pressing them through.

Mix again, and pour into one greased 9x13 inch pan. Tap the edge of the pan against the edge of the counter to pop air bubbles. Bake at 350 for 25-30 minutes. Serves 8.

RASPBERRY COULIS

1 ½ cups fresh raspberries or 10 oz bag of frozen berries
¼ cup brown rice syrup, honey, or brown sugar
½ teaspoon vanilla

Puree in a food processor or blender. Add water if needed. You want a thick sauce that is still easy to pour. Drizzle on top of the cake or spoon on the bottom of the plate and put cake on top.

Vegan Chocolate Cake continued...

CHOCOLATE SAUCE

1 ½ cups maple syrup
3 tablespoons light vegetable oil
2 cups cocoa powder, sifted
1 teaspoon vanilla

In a 2-quart saucepan heat together sweetener and oil. Whisk in the cocoa powder. Simmer for several minutes–fewer minutes for sauce, more for icing. Turn off heat and stir in the vanilla.

TO ASSEMBLE

Pour 1 tablespoon of raspberry coulis at the bottom of a dessert plate. Let the coulis cover about ½ of the plate (enough so you can see the coulis when you put the cake on top of it). Place cake on the coulis and drizzle chocolate sauce on top of cake. Garnish cake with a fresh mint leaf and a raspberry.

◇◇

THE GOO!

Otherwise known as German chocolate cake topping, this gooey stuff on top of the vegan chocolate cake recipe is over the top…YUM!!!

4 large egg yolks
1 cup sugar
2 cups whole milk
¼ cup light brown sugar
6 tablespoons unsalted butter
⅛ teaspoon sea salt
2 teaspoons vanilla extract
2 ½ cups unsweetened shredded coconut
1 ½ cups chopped and toasted pecans

Whisk yolk, sugars, and milk in a saucepan. Heat to a simmer on medium heat. Add butter and sea salt. Simmer while whisking until the mixture is frothy and thickened, about 6 minutes. Transfer to a bowl and whisk in vanilla, then stir in coconut. Cool until just warm and refrigerate. Add pecans when you are about to frost the cake. Makes 6 cups.

WILD FOODS

CHESTNUT CAKE WITH CANDY CAP GLAZE

CANDY CAP CRÈME BRULE

CANDY CAP COCONUT TAPIOCA

NETTLE SOUP

BACON NETTLE GOAT CHEVRE QUICHE
WITH A MILLET ALMOND CRUST

SAGE AND WILD MUSHROOM RISOTTO

GOAT CHEESE TART WITH HEDGEHOG
MUSHROOMS AND A MEYER LEMON CRUST

CHESTNUT CAKE *with* CANDY CAP GLAZE *and* WHIPPED CREAM

This Italian influenced dessert is one of my all-time favorite recipes. This cake is both sweet and savory. You can find chestnut flour at your health food store or online. Candy cap mushrooms are found at specialty markets, online, or harvested by you (of course).

Chestnuts were once prolific in the United States. The chestnut was called "the grain that grows on trees," and they say that a squirrel could travel on chestnut trees from the east coast all the way to the Mississippi never touching the ground. In the 1930's, a blight came and wiped out the entire American chestnut population. Prodigal Summer, *by Barbara Kingsolver, is a great book to learn more about the American chestnut.*

CHESTNUT CAKE

1 ½ cups chestnut flour
1 ½ cups white spelt flour or unbleached white flour
1 ½ tablespoon baking powder
½ teaspoon sea salt
¼ cup extra-virgin olive oil
¼ cup light vegetable oil
1 cup brown rice syrup or honey
1 ½ cups soymilk, goat milk, or whole milk
Zest and juice of an orange
1 tablespoon fresh rosemary chopped, or ½ teaspoon dried, minced
¼ cup pine nuts lightly toasted

To make the cake: preheat the oven to 350 degrees. Grease two 9-inch cake pans. In a large bowl, mix dry ingredients. In a medium bowl, whisk together wet ingredients, then stir into dry ingredients with whisk until evenly moistened. Fold in pine nuts. Transfer batter to cake pans and bake until golden (about 30 minutes), or until cake tests done with a clean knife or toothpick.

To serve, pour 1 tablespoon candy cap glaze on a plate, place cake on it, and top with whipped cream and a few toasted pinenuts. Serves 6-8.

Chestnut Cake recipe continues on the following page...

CANDY CAP GLAZE

½ cup sugar
¼ cup water
1 tablespoon ground candy cap mushrooms
1 fresh vanilla pod, cut open and scraped

In a pot, boil the sugar, water, ground mushrooms, vanilla pod and scrapings for 5 minutes. Pull out the vanilla pod and let cool.

OPTION

If you don't have candy cap mushrooms, add one extra vanilla stick to this recipe.

WHIPPED CREAM

1 cup cold heavy cream
2 tablespoons brown sugar
½ teaspoon vanilla

Whip all the ingredients together with a hand blender or whisk until it becomes the consistency you like.

CANDY CAP CRÈME BRULE

FOR CUSTARD

2 cups whipping cream
½ cup sugar
½ cup whole dried candy cap mushrooms, chopped fine
1 vanilla bean, split lengthwise
5 egg yolks

FOR CRÈME BRULE

12 teaspoons sugar

TO MAKE CUSTARD

Preheat oven to 325 degrees. Place six ¾ cup ramekins in a casserole dish. Using a small knife, scrape the "caviar" from the vanilla bean

Mix cream, sugar, candy caps, vanilla caviar and pod together in a heavy bottomed saucepan. Gently bring to a boil while stirring, reduce heat. Cover pot and simmer for 15 minutes. Strain mixture through a fine mesh strainer.

Whisk yolk in a medium sized bowl until blended. Temper the eggs by pouring 2 tablespoons of hot cream mixture at a time while mixing the eggs. This prevents the eggs from scrambling.

Measure ½ cup of mixture into each ramekin. In the casserole dish, pour hot water so that it comes ½ way up the sides of the ramekins.

Bake custards until almost set when the ramekins are gently shaken, about 35 minutes.

Using a metal spatula, transfer custards onto a work surface. Let cool 30 minutes then put in the refrigerator to chill 3 hours or up to 2 days.

TO MAKE CRÈME BRULE

Sprinkle 2 teaspoons sugar evenly over each custard. Working with one ramekin at a time, hold blowtorch* so the flame is 2 inches above the surface and move the flame in a circular manner. The flame melts and browns the sugar in about 2 minutes. Alternatively, preheat the broiler/grill and slip the custards under the broiler 4 to 6 inches from the heat source to melt the sugar; leave the oven door open slightly and watch closely, as the sugar can scorch suddenly.

Refrigerate the custards until the topping is brittle and the custard is firm again, about 1-2 hours (but no longer than 4 hours to avoid the top getting soft).

*You can get great butane blowtorches at many cookware stores.

CANDY CAP COCONUT TAPIOCA

Tapioca is an easy treat to make. The secret is having enough time to stir. I like to use agave as a tapioca sweetener, because it is mild and delicious. Candy cap mushrooms (Lactarius rubidus) are amongst my favorite of all the local wild mushrooms. To me, their flavor is a mix of maple syrup and earth. When dry, one single candy cap mushroom can fill an entire room with its smell. I like to use dried candy caps in desserts and savory dishes. It may sound weird to put mushrooms in dessert, but try it. Really.

2 cups water
2 cups coconut milk
¼ cup agave syrup, honey, brown rice syrup or sugar
1 tablespoon maple syrup
1 teaspoon ground dried candy cap powder
¼ teaspoon sea salt
½ cup small tapioca pearls
1 teaspoon vanilla

Place coconut milk, water, agave, maple, candy cap powder and salt in a saucepan. Bring to a boil. Add tapioca. Turn heat down and simmer uncovered until the pearls are almost all transparent, about 25-30 minutes. Stir every 2 minutes or so. Remove from heat and stir in vanilla. Adjust sweetness to your liking. The tapioca will continue to thicken as it cools.

VARIATION

Remove the candy caps and add ½ cup semi-sweet chocolate chips to the tapioca to make chocolate coconut tapioca. Serves 4.

EAT SOMETHING WILD EVERYDAY

I like to eat foods that want to grow of their own accord, uncultivated, in between the cracks in the sidewalk or out in the woods. They want to live. They know how to survive. I like wild foods because they stick close to their nature. We are what we eat after all, and if we always eat domesticated and cultivated foods, we lose some of our own resilience along the way.

There is stuff to know when you forage for wild foods. There are plenty of wild edibles out there, but you need to know how, when, and which part to eat them. You want to learn any dangerous look-a-likes. Please do not start putting random plants on your dinner plate. But DO learn! There is a world of plants to explore, including in your own back yard.

One of the most delicious wild edibles is stinging nettles. Yes, stinging nettles. Nettles have long been an important wild green in many cultures. They have been used for food, medicine, cloth fibers, and dyes. High in digestible iron, nettles rival any dark leafy green in terms of nutrition.

Nettles are rich and delicious. Pick them with gloves on (or if you dare, barehanded), then steam, blanch, or sauté them and the stingers will go away. In the springtime, they like to grow in moist, shady areas, often near creeks. I have my favorite nettle picking grounds that I keep secret. Since the seeds contain a lot of silica, which is difficult to digest, only eat them before they have gone to seed (not after). Cook them as you would cook Swiss chard or spinach.

NETTLE SOUP

Bright green is the color of this soup. You can ask a farmer friend if they have any nettles, or find your own special patch.

8 cups nettle leaves
2 tablespoons unsalted butter
1 yellow onion, diced
1 yukon gold potato, peeled and diced
6 cups baby spinach leaves
1 ½ teaspoon sea salt
6 cups water or vegetarian stock
½ cup cream (optional)

Bring 8 cups of water to a boil. Wearing gloves, dunk the nettles into the hot water for 2 minutes to blanch them (blanching removes the stingers). Drain, remove any large stems, and chop. Melt butter in a soup pot. Add onion and potato. Sauté about 5 minutes. Add spinach, sea salt and water. Bring to a boil. Add the nettles. Simmer for about 15 minutes.

Puree the soup. Return to low heat. Add the cream. Adjust the salt to taste. Serves 6-8.

BACON NETTLE GOAT CHEVRE QUICHE *with a* MILLET ALMOND CRUST

CRUST

½ cup millet
½ cup almonds
1 cup spelt flour or unbleached white flour
½ cup butter
Water

Heat oven to 350 degrees. In a food processor, grind the almonds to a rough flour. In a bowl, mix the millet, almond flour and spelt flour together. Cut the butter into 1 inch cubes and put in to mix. Using two butter knives or a pastry cutter, continue to cut up the butter in the flour until there are pea-sized pieces of butter. Add water 1 tablespoon at a time, until the mixture holds together. Butter the bottom of the pan. Press the crust into the bottom of a pie pan. Pre-bake the crust for 10 minutes.

THE FILLING

4 eggs
¼ cup arrowroot powder
1 cup milk or goat milk
½ cup heavy cream
1 teaspoon sea salt
¼ teaspoon nutmeg
2 slices of bacon, fried and cut into bite sized pieces
½ cup sautéed nettles (or chard)
½ cup onions, sautéed
¼ cup goat chevre
2 tablespoons shredded Parmesan

In a separate bowl, mix the eggs, arrowroot, milk, cream, salt and nutmeg. At the bottom of your pre-baked crust, spread the bacon, nettles, goat chevre and Parmesan evenly over the bottom. Pour the egg mixture over the top. Bake in an oven at 350 for 30 minutes until the mixture is set and the center is just a little soft. Let cool and serve at room temperature. Serves 6-8.

OPTION

For a vegetarian option, remove the bacon and add 1 chopped tomato to the recipe.

SAGE *and* WILD MUSHROOM RISOTTO

Every winter, I go foraging for mushrooms on the Sonoma Coast. It is truly my favorite winter activity. I am obsessed. There is nothing like being face-down on the forest floor, limbs spread in all directions, finding delicious, edible, wild mushrooms. It's the greatest treasure hunt ever. It's taken some time to learn which ones are edible and which ones are not. If you are interested in learning more, check out your local mycological society.

About 8 fresh sage leaves, or 1 tablespoon dried
1 medium onion
8 cups chicken stock or un-chicken stock
5 ½ tablespoons unsalted butter or olive oil
2 cups Arborio rice
½ cup dry white wine (optional)
¼ pound mushrooms (black trumpet, oyster, hedgehog, shitake, crimini), sliced
Salt and pepper
½ cup grated Parmesan cheese

Chop 8 fresh sage leaves fine and cut the onion into small dice. Heat the chicken stock and keep at a low simmer. In another heavy-bottomed saucepan, heat 3 tablespoons of the butter, add the chopped sage, and cook for a minute or so. Add the onion and continue to cook over medium heat until it is translucent, about 3 minutes. Add the mushrooms and sauté for 3 minutes.

Add the rice and a pinch of salt, and cook over low heat for about 3 minutes, stirring often, until the rice has turned slightly translucent. Turn up the heat and pour in the white wine. When the wine has been absorbed, add just enough stock to cover the rice, stir well, and reduce the heat. Keep the rice at a gentle simmer and continue to add more stock, a ladle or two at a time, letting each addition be absorbed by the rice. While the rice is cooking, sauté the remaining sage leaves in butter until crisp. After 15 minutes, the rice will be nearly cooked. Stir in 2 ½ tablespoons butter, and the cheese. Continue cooking for 3 to 5 minutes. Taste for texture and consistency, adding a little more stock if needed. Adjust the seasoning. When done, serve in warm bowls and garnish with extra cheese and olive oil. Serves 6.

The Mushroom Song:
I love mushrooms, I love mushrooms, I love mushrooms, Ohhh Ohhh...They are soft, they are spongy, and slimy too. (repeat)

GOAT CHEESE TART *with* HEDGEHOG MUSHROOMS *and* MEYER LEMON CRUST

This tart incorporates my favorite things about winter: goat cheese, wild mushrooms, and Meyer lemons. If you don't have hedgehog mushrooms, you can use black trumpet mushrooms, yellow feet mushrooms or regular button mushrooms from the store.

1 (9-inch) homemade spelt tart crust
3 large leeks
2 tablespoon unsalted butter
6 ounces goat cheese
1 egg
½ cup crème fraiche
½ cup milk
1 cup hedgehog mushrooms, whole if small, chopped if large
Sea salt and white pepper
2 teaspoons chopped thyme leaves

TART FILLING

Preheat the oven to 400 degrees. Slice the leeks in to rounds, separate them, then wash well and strain. Melt 1 tablespoon butter in a skillet. Add leeks and cook till tender, 10 minutes. Season with sea salt and pepper. Remove from skillet and set aside.

Add 1 tablespoon of butter to skillet and melt over medium heat. Add mushrooms and cook on medium heat till soft, about 5 minutes. Beat the goat cheese with the egg until smooth. Add the milk, crème fraiche, salt, and white pepper and stir.

Line the bottom of the crust with the leeks and mushrooms. Pour the mushroom custard over this. Bake until golden, about 30 minutes. Garnish with thyme leaves and Meyer lemon zest. Transfer to a serving platter. Serve warm. Serves 8.

MEYER LEMON CRUST

1 cup plus 2 tablespoons white spelt flour or all-purpose flour
⅛ teaspoon sea salt
½ cup (one stick) unsalted butter, in chunks
2-3 tablespoons ice water
Zest from one Meyer lemon (optional)

Using a mixer with a paddle attachment (or a food processor), blend the flour, salt and sugar and zest, and then work in butter until coarse crumbs are formed. Add just enough ice water for the dough to come together. Shape into a ball. Wrap in plastic and chill for 20 minutes.

Roll the dough into a 10-inch circle and lay over a 9-inch tart pan with the removable rim (or a pie pan). The dough should be ¼ inch above the rim and about ¼ inch thick. Prick the bottom with a fork several times then freeze for 30 minutes. Preheat the oven to 425 degrees. Place frozen tart in oven for 25 minutes, until it's lightly colored. Fix any holes with extra pastry scraps.

TEAS

HIBISCUS COOLER

ANISE CINNAMON TEA

CHAMOMILE ROSEHIP GARDEN TEA

ROSE LAVENDER MINT TEA

JODIE'S CHAI

ROSEMARY MINT TEA WITH HONEY

STAR ANISE VANILLA TEA WITH ROOIBOS

HIBISCUS COOLER

I like to serve this lightly sweetened drink when kids are around. Hibiscus is tasty, has a great color, and is high in vitamin C.

2 cups water
3 tablespoons dried hibiscus flowers
¼ cup sugar
6 cups cold water

Boil 2 cups of water. Reduce heat, add hibiscus and let simmer for 1 minute. Turn off flame. Add sugar and stir. Let concentrate infuse for 10 minutes. Strain the concentrate and let cool. Add 6 cups cold water. Refrigerate. Serves 8.

OPTION

You can substitute 4 tablespoons apple or raspberry concentrate for sugar.

ANISE CINNAMON TEA

This is a great after dinner tea. It can be served hot or cold. Anise and cinnamon are both naturally sweet and supportive to digestion.

4 cups water
1 teaspoon anise seeds
2 whole cinnamon sticks

In a pot place water, anise, and cinnamon. Bring to a boil, reduce heat, and let simmer for 20 minutes. Strain the spices and serve. Serves 4.

OPTION

Add 5-7 pine nuts to each cup for an unusual twist to the tea.

CHAMOMILE-ROSEHIP GARDEN TEA

This is a good infusion to calm and nourish the nerves and muscles, and the vitamin C in the rosehips is good for the immune system. These two recipes were developed by RDI neighbor Kyra Epstein, master of herbal tea formulas and owner of Gaia Blends tea company.

2 cups water
2 tablespoons fresh chamomile flowers (or 2 teaspoons dried)
1 tablespoon fresh raspberry leaves (or 1 teaspoon dried)
1 tablespoon rose hips, chopped or crushed

Bring water almost to a boil and turn off the heat. Rough chop chamomile flowers and raspberry leaves. Stir in plants and cover pot with a lid to steep for 3-5 minutes.

Strain and enjoy with or without honey. Serves 2.

To contact Kyra about her teas, email her at gaiateablends@gmail.com.

ROSE-LAVENDER MINT TEA

This tea blends the delicate beauty of these garden flowers with the vibrant, digestive-aiding mint.

2 cups water
1 or 2 long sprigs mint
½ cup fresh rose petals
2 sprigs lavender flowers

Bring water almost to a boil. Turn off the heat.

Curl stalks of your favorite mint (rinsed) into the pan, along with rose petals (also rinsed). Cover pan and let steep for 5 minutes.

Strain into mugs, and add a sprig of lavender to the mug. Enjoy with or without honey. Serves 2.

JODIE'S CHAI

3 cups water
2 inch piece of fresh ginger, sliced (if you don't like it too spicy, put in less ginger)
1 cinnamon stick
2 tablespoons fennel or anise seed
2 tablespoons green cardamom pods, crushed
5 black peppercorns
2½ cups of milk (cow's milk is suggested, but goat milk is also traditionally used)
1½ tablespoons sugar (adjust according to your taste)
2 tablespoons black tea (rooibos tea or decaffeinated black tea
can be substituted for a caffeine-free version)

DIRECTIONS

In a pot, combine water, fresh ginger, cinnamon, fennel, cardamom and black peppercorns. Bring to a boil. Once the water is at a steady boil, add milk and sugar. Bring back to a boil and then down to a simmer for about 10 minutes. This allows for the milk to reduce and for the sugars to caramelize—this is the secret!

Keep your eye on the stove, the milk tends to boil over, so as soon as it begins to boil, turn down the heat and stir.

After 10 minutes, add your tea, whichever you've chosen, and continue to simmer for another 7-10 minutes. Strain in a mesh tea strainer and enjoy!

SIDE NOTE

You always want to bring the fresh ginger root to a boil before you add your milk. If the ginger hasn't already been up to a boil, your milk will curdle when you pour it in. If you're in a rush and don't have time to bring your spices to a full boil, then leave out the ginger or use powdered ginger instead. Makes 4 cups.

ROSEMARY MINT TEA *with* HONEY

4 cups water
3 inch sprig of fresh rosemary or 1 tablespoon dry rosemary
2 sprigs fresh mint or 2 teaspoons dry mint
Honey

Bring water to a boil. Add rosemary and let simmer for 5 minutes. Turn off the heat and add mint. Let steep for 5 minutes. Add honey to taste. Serves 4.

Nikon

STAR ANISE VANILLA TEA *with* ROOIBOS

This is a mock Thai ice tea. The rooibos adds a nice natural color and flavor. I love it just as it is, but you can also add milk/coconut milk if you wish.

2 sticks fresh vanilla pods
6 cups water
6 star anise pods
6 whole cloves
3 sticks cinnamon
3 tablespoons sugar, agave or honey
2 tablespoons rooibos

Open and scrape out the vanilla center from the vanilla pod. In a pot, add water, vanilla (pod and scrapings), star anise, cloves, cinnamon and sweetener. Bring to a boil and let simmer for 20-30 minutes. Turn off heat and add rooibos. Let steep for 5 minutes. Strain. Save the star anise and put one in each cup. Serve hot or cold. Makes 5 cups.

OPTIONS

Substitute 2 cups coconut milk or whole milk for 2 cups water and let boil with the spices.

< *Drying herbs in a solar dehydrator.*

HERBAL FIRST AID

take 5 Drosera drops or
lizing Cordial every
hydrated/ Replace loss with
e.o.rubbed onto abdomen/

FIRST AID KIT

I always have some first aid essentials on-hand in the kitchen for burns, cuts, body pains and general stress. My first aid kit contains a mixture of western, eastern, and herbal medicine. While I don't have space to share why I choose to have these remedies and not others, I wanted to give you a sense of what I keep on hand to inspire you to flesh out your first aid kit. This list is not an endorsement of any kind, just one cook sharing the items she has on hand for first aid in the kitchen. You can get most of these items at a health food store or a drug store.

On the farm, we get to make our own lavender essential oils and hydrosols with Penny's alembic. We also collect propolis from the bees. There are some excellent courses at the farm about herbal medicines and how to make them. If you're interested, check out the RDI website for details.

HERE IS A LIST OF WHAT I ALWAYS KEEP ON HAND

Band aids (all different sizes)
Cotton balls
Tweezers
Thermometer
Latex gloves (to protect any cuts you may have on your hands)
Finger cots (to protect any cuts you may have on your finger)
Hot water bottle (for cold feet and stomach upsets)
Isotonic sea-salt solution (sore throats)
Arnica (bruises)
Lavender essential oil (stress and burns)
Lavender aloe burn spray (burns)
Peppermint essential oil (congestion and stomach upsets)
Propolis (sore throats)
Larrea tincture (inflammation, aches, body pain)
Homeopathic burn tablets (burns)
Homeopathic sleep aid
Osho root, Echinacea, Usnea (antibiotic tincture)
Elderflower yarrow tea (for colds)
Herbal expectorant (cough)
Senna Pills (constipation)
Comfrey salve (to protect any cuts/wounds)
Skullcap tincture (to calm stress)
Yarrow leaf powder (to stop bleeding on small cuts)
Tiger balm (back pain)
Umeboshi plums (to balance out blood sugar imbalances due to excessive sugar or alcohol)
Kudzu root (indigestion)
Clay (poison oak remedy)
Aspirin (headaches)
Ibuprofen (aches and inflammation)
Triple antibiotic cream (cuts)
The Curing pill (digestive woes)
Cold Snap (preventative cold medicine)
Yin Ciao (preventative cold medicine)
Rescue Remedy (stress)

NOTE

The first aid kit you see in the photo was created by master herbalists and medicine-makers Jasmyn Clift and Kevin Kunzler at their Wildseed School of Herbal Medicine on Salt Spring Island, Canada. It is one of my most prized possessions. If you are interested in investing in a powerful herbal first aid kit of your own, you can contact Kevin at sandhillbotanical@gmail.com, or check out their site www.wildseedschool.com.

GLOSSARY

ARROWROOT

Arrowroot is a white powdery starch that can be substituted for cornstarch in a lot of recipes. Arrowroot makes clear, shimmering fruit gels and prevents ice crystals from forming in homemade ice cream. It can also be used as a thickener for acidic foods, such as Asian sweet and sour sauce, or used in cooking to produce a clear, thickened sauce, such as a fruit sauce. (Cornstarch would make the fruit sauce cloudy.)

BROWN RICE SYRUP

Brown rice syrup is a delicious sticky sweetener derived by culturing cooked rice with enzymes (usually from dried barley sprouts) to break down the starches, then straining off the liquid and cooking it until the desired consistency is reached. It is often used as a liquid sweetener in baking, and can be a substitute for honey.

CALIFORNIA BAY LEAVES

The California bay tree is also known as California laurel, Oregon myrtle, and pepperwood. It is similar to the Mediterranean bay laurel, but has a stronger flavor and smell. California bay trees grow everywhere in California, and I prefer to use local bay leaves in my cooking.

FISH SAUCE

Fish Sauce is commonly used in Thai and Southeast Asian cooking, however it does have a place in ancient Roman cooking too! Most fish sauces are made from raw fish, most from only a single species of fish, like anchovies. Most fish sauces contain only fish, water and salt. While fish sauce smells and tastes intense on its own, it adds a delicious flavor to many Asian dishes, like authentic Thai curry. The brand I like is "Three Crabs" fish sauce, and you can find it in the Asian markets. It usually costs three bucks or so. I advise you to spend the extra money to have a glass bottle and a decent lid on your fish sauce. Believe me, you don't want to spill that bottle.

GALANGAL

This delicious root is a rhizome of plants in the ginger family Zingiberaceaee, with culinary and medicinal uses originating in Indonesia. The rhizomes are used in various Asian cuisines (for example in Thai curry and tom kha gai soups). Though it is related to ginger and resembles it in appearance, there is little similarity in taste. Galangal has a more floral flavor than ginger, and it is not hot.

KAFFIR LIME LEAVES

These aromatic leaves are used in Thai cooking and Southeast Asian cuisine. The rinds are often used in Thai curry paste, and the juice is used as a cleanser for clothing and hair in Thailand. Kaffir grows well in the greenhouse at RDI.

MIRIN

Mirin is an essential condiment used in Japanese cooking. It is a rice wine similar to sake, but with a lower alcohol content. Sweet with a yummy flavor, mirin is used to make teriyaki sauce and sushi, and can flavor other sauces.

MISO

Miso is a salty fermented paste that has been fermented anywhere from five days to several years. Miso is essential in any kitchen. Miso is often made from a mix of fermented soy beans, barley, rice, buckwheat, millet, rye, wheat, and hemp seed. Miso paste is used for culinary as well as medicinal reasons.

POMEGRANATE MOLASSES

Pomegranate molasses is not really molasses, but a syrup made from the reduced fruit of pomegranate seeds. Used in Persian cooking, pomegranate molasses has a distinctive sweet and sour flavor, and a lovely deep red color. Look for it in your health food store or Middle Eastern markets.

RICE OIL

Otherwise known as rice bran oil, rice oil is made from the bran of the rice hull. Often used in South Asian cooking, rice oil has a high smoke point and is great for deep-frying. It has similar cooking properties as peanut oil. I like to use rice oil in baking, as it is flavorless. High in anti-oxidants, rice bran oil has been shown in studies in Japan to reduce hot flashes in menopausal women.

SEA SALT

Sea salt comes from evaporating seawater. Sea salt contains trace minerals, including iodine. It has the same sodium chloride composition as mined mineral salt, but without the additives and anti-clumping agents. Many say sea salt is energetically healthier than mined salt. Mined salt is baked at very high temperatures, eliminating important trace minerals. Sea salt is created with natural solar evaporation.

SMOKED PAPRIKA

Smoked paprika comes from paprika peppers being dried through smoking with oak wood. Smoked paprika imparts a delicious flavor and natural color to your food, and it is often used in Spanish cooking.

SPELT FLOUR

Spelt is an heirloom variety of wheat cultivated over 8,000 years ago. Spelt can be used as an excellent substitute for wheat in most recipes. Spelt flour in cookies, cakes, pastry, and bread all substitute one for one with wheat flour. For those wanting less gluten, but enjoy the taste and texture of wheat, spelt can be a great option.

SUMAC

Sumac is a purple red spice from the Rhea family. It is commonly used in Turkish, Moroccan, and Iranian cooking. Its sweet and sour flavor is used to flavor salad and meats, and is an excellent garnish for hummus. It is a main ingredient in zatar as well.

ROOSTER SAUCE

Otherwise known as Shri Racha, rooster sauce is a hot and sour red sauce thought to originate from the town of Si Racha in central Thailand. Used to garnish Thai food, rooster sauce brings a great flavor to curries and pad thai. Rooster sauce contains chili, sugar, vinegar, garlic, and salt and can be found at Asian markets. It has a rooster on the bottle.

ZATAR

A common spice mix found on the table in many Middle-Eastern countries. The proportions of thyme, sumac and sesame seeds in zatar varies from place to place.

THANK YOU

Thank you to RDI (and your goats, gardens and bees) and Commonweal Garden for your inspiration to create this project. Thank you all the people who have eaten food with me, and specific thanks to: Penny Livingston, James Stark, Erin O'Reilly, Michael Rauner, Caroline Wallace, Max Rosenblum, Paz de la Calzada, Kirk Read, Teo Weiss, Taylor Ray, Kelly Akashi, Madrone Jack, Starhawk, Frances Carati, the Pigeon Palace, Charles Williams, Shanna Lopresti, Robert Hickling, Jodie Kleeman, Nora Vitaliani, Jeremy Peckham, Wowzer, Evan Rottman, Ryan Mesch, Bela Growdon, Alcina Horstman, Chris Carlsson, Adriana Camarena, Lisa Ruth, Giorgio Anthony, Kristen Wood, Nick Venegoni, Pamela Rosin, Tom Greybalt, Tasha Berg, Kyra Epstein, Fyn Sidian, Sayre, Bridgid Kneadstir, Jasmyn Clift, Kevin Kunzler, Jacob Nasim, Lisa Mekis, Leah Spinrad, and Helen Hawk. Your support and encouragement has meant the world in helping this project come to life.

Culinary Magic: www.culinarymagic.com
Regenerative Design Institute: www.regenerativedesign.org
Commonweal: www.commonweal.org
Design: Caroline Wallace (www.carolinewallacedesign.com)
Production Design: Kelly Akashi (www.kellyakashidesign.com)
Photography: Michael Rauner (www.michaelrauner.com), and Caroline Wallace

Carin McKay lives in San Francisco, California.

INDEX

T

V

W

Y

Z

Photo credits by page:

Michael Rauner: Front cover, 8, 9, 10, 11, 13, 14, 15, 18, 20, 21, 22, 23, 27, 28, 29, 31, 35, 36, 42, 54, 56, 60, 64, 66, 68, 92, 94, 98, 108 (bottom L and R), 113, 116, 117, 119, 120, 132, 134, 141, 144, 148, 154, 172, 174, 180, 182, 184, 189, 190, 191.

Caroline Wallace: Back cover, 7, 17, 25, 32, 44, 48, 70, 72, 76, 78, 80, 84, 96, 103, 106, 108 (top R and L), 122, 124, 138, 143, 152, 156, 162, 166, 168, 176.